Overextended

"Jesus did not come so we could have a safe-picket-fence life. In her book *Overextended . . . and Loving Most of It!*, Lisa challenges and encourages us to live the big life that God designed for us to live. In her practical and oh-so-funny way she paints the picture of how we really can live our everyday life in a way that honors God and makes a difference in the world. You will love this book . . . really!!!"

—Holly Wagner
Founder and Author of *GodChicks*, *Warrior Chicks*, and *Survival Guide for Young Women*

"Lisa Harper is a true gift to everyone who knows her. This book gives you an opportunity to hear from a woman who not only talks it, but walks it. I know a lot of people who read and quote the Bible. Lisa not only knows the words, she also knows what they mean, and why *those* words were used instead of others. She's funny, bright, dedicated, and an absolute BLAST to hang out with. Read this book!"

—Scott Hamilton
Olympic Gold Medalist

"I have known this whirlwind of a woman, Lisa Harper, for many years. And here's the scoop: she's the real deal. Lisa hot-foot's the gospel around the world and her fervor is contagious, as is her obvious passion for words that sizzle with truth. I love Lisa, as will you—catch the fire of living life with a full heart!"

—Patsy Clairmont
Author of *Twirl*

"I love a book that's funny, honest, challenging, biblical, heartfelt, and real, real, real. *Overextended . . . and Loving Most of It!* is just that kind of read. Lisa walks us through the mountain tops and valley depths of living *all in* for Jesus, using personal stories and biblical wisdom to drive home truths we all need to hear. A great read!"

—Liz Curtis Higgs
Best-Selling Author of *Bad Girls of the Bible* and *The Girl's Still Got It*

"Lisa's writing is just like sitting across the table from her. One minute you're holding your stomach because you're laughing so hard, and the next thing you know you're wiping away tears because she's just said something beautiful and inspiring and poignant. Lisa makes you want to live life out loud in all the fullness that God has for us. You will find inspiration and laughter in every word and walk away feeling like you've just said good-bye to a dear friend."

—MELANIE SHANKLE
AUTHOR OF *SPARKLY GREEN EARRINGS*

"The first thing you'll learn about Lisa Harper is that she has a huge heart. She's approachable while being honest and funny while teaching sometimes hard life lessons. One of the greatest gifts Lisa gives to the world is her ability to transform stories from the Bible we all know into fresh and relatable truth. You will be challenged, you will laugh a lot, and you will occasionally shed a tear. But most importantly, you will grow closer to God and feel empowered in your faith. I love Lisa Harper, and I know you will too."

—SANDI PATTY
GRAMMY AND DOVE AWARD-WINNING SINGER

"Out of Lisa's overextended life emerges a collection of unforgettable lessons. Thankfully she has assembled them so the rest of us can benefit. Slow down. Take a breath and enjoy this book!"

—MAX LUCADO
PASTOR AND BEST-SELLING AUTHOR

"In order to do what God has called us to do we must ensure that we only do what He has called us to do. In *Overextended* Lisa shows us how to live this awesome faith adventure constantly stretching ourselves but not snapping in the process. This is a timely and much needed message for the body of Christ."

—CHRISTINE CAINE
FOUNDER OF THE A21 CAMPAIGN

Overextended

...and loving most of it!

The Unexpected Joy of Being
Harried, Heartbroken, and Hurling
Oneself Off Cliffs

LISA HARPER

W PUBLISHING GROUP

AN IMPRINT OF THOMAS NELSON

Published in Nashville, Tennessee, by Thomas Nelson. Thomas Nelson is a registered trademark of Thomas Nelson, Inc.

Lisa Harper is represented by Anvil II Management.

Thomas Nelson, Inc., titles may be purchased in bulk for educational, business, fund-raising, or sales promotional use. For information, please e-mail SpecialMarkets@ThomasNelson.com.

Library of Congress Cataloging-in-Publication Data Available Upon Request

ISBN 978-0-8499-2192-6

Printed in the United States of America

13 14 15 16 17 18 RRD 6 5 4 3 2

In loving memory of my father,
Everett Andrew Harper, who is probably
riding a horse and roping a steer in
Glory at this very moment.
I miss you, Dad.

TABLE OF CONTENTS

"We are surrounded by a great cloud of people whose lives tell us what faith means. So let us run the race that is before us and never give up."

—Hebrews 12:1a NCV

FOREWORD

I feel morally obliged to begin with a disclaimer: I simply adore Lisa Harper! We have been friends for over twenty years, and as the years have passed that friendship has deepened into a lifelong commitment to be there for one another, no matter what. I don't think either of us realized years ago just how deep that "what" might be. How could we have known in the earlier days of ministry that God would stretch us in ways that at times would make it hard to catch our breath?

I have watched the unfolding of Lisa's life and at times I've had to remind myself to breathe as she is stretched in ways that, as her sister and friend, make me want to shout, "Stop!" But with every stretching I have seen it. I have watched the tender outpouring of fresh grace and the profound intensifying of her allegiance to Christ and

....

His people. I have watched her say, *"Yes!"* over and over, not to the pressures of a culture that would consume but to a Savior who would transform. Lisa does not live safely. She lives a full-out, pedal to the metal, cross the finish line dripping with sweat and tears and laughter, kind of life.

If you're tempted to think that this all sounds a bit too much, a bit "unhealthy," I would say this: there are two ways to live that could fall under the heading "Overextended."

There is one where no boundaries are in place. Many well-meaning followers of Christ lie bleeding on this road. They have tried to please everyone around them and martyred their joy on the cross of the approval of others. I have traveled this road and it almost killed me. This path is hard, and graceless, and full of potholes.

This is not the path that Lisa writes about in these pages. There is another way to live an "overextended" life.

The life that I watch my friend embrace reminds me of the life Paul lived, recorded in the book of Acts.

But I do not account my life of any value nor as precious to myself, if only I may finish my course and the ministry that I received from the Lord Jesus, to testify to the gospel of the grace of God. (Acts 20:24)

. . . .

This is a life worth living! It's a life that's exhausting and exhilarating, heartbreaking and soaked to the skin with the beauty of redemptive grace.

Lisa's story is far from over, but what a gift to be invited to join her at this place, at this time, and see what Christ will do in and through a life sold-out to Him.

You will love Lisa's stories and, yes, some will make you shake your head in disbelief unless you know Lisa. Then, of course, they will make perfect sense.

You will love Lisa's heart and want to pull in a little closer.

More than that, you might find yourself taking a look at your own life and deciding to risk a little more, to love more passionately so that when you reach the finish line you too are . . . *breathless!*

—Sheila Walsh
Author of *God Loves Broken People*

1

LIVING A JESUS WAY OF LIFE

Tell me, what is it you plan to do with
your one wild and precious life?[1]

—*Mary Oliver*

March 27, 2013

S oon after I woke up this morning, I wanted to kick
Eve in the shins. After six months of no *visits from
my uncle*, no *time of the month*—or as our fifth
grade PE teacher so indelicately referred to it, no MEN-
STRU-A-TION cycles—now it chooses to appear in full
glory while I'm staying at a guesthouse in a third-world

country without any supplies or a Walgreens around the corner! Ugh. While I'm a tad grateful this proves I'm not in full-blown menopause yet—especially since I'm about to become a first-time mom (which I'll explain later)—I'm not at all happy about having to deal with this today, when I'll be spending the majority of it waiting around in hot, overcrowded Haitian government offices with no restroom facilities.

So after I finished my coffee I carefully approached Madame Suzette, the beautiful and gracious proprietress of the guesthouse and asked tentatively if she had any "feminine supplies." It was the beginning of a stilted, awkward conversation because like many of the Haitians I've met, Madame Suzette is very reserved and dignified . . . especially when it comes to personal matters. And here I was trampling propriety less than forty-eight hours after arriving from America. To complicate matters, her English is heavily accented and my Creole is horrible, so it took a lot of gesturing and repetition before she said, "Oui, oui" and seemed to comprehend that I needed "private products." She nodded to one of her assistants standing meekly behind her and said something in Creole, to which the young woman responded "Oui, Madame" and scurried off—presumably to retrieve the unmentionables.

Then Madame Suzette turned her attention back to me and said politely but haltingly, "Your. Hair. Looks.

Very . . . *belle* (the Creole word for "beautiful") theeze morning." I replied, "*Mesi boukou* (thank you very much)." She continued by asking, "Do you use thee long wans or thee short wans?" And I replied, "Pardon me, madame?" I wasn't sure exactly what she meant by the question. So we started playing charades again and this time she motioned her hands to symbolize a long, thin tube while repeating slowly and emphatically, "Do. You. Use. Thee. Long. Wan?" And I recognized in a flash that she wanted to know if I used a flat iron. You know us girls; hair is always at the forefront of our conversations!

Frankly, I was quite flattered by her curiosity about my styling regimen because I didn't think my hair looked that great in light of the heat and humidity. So I grinned with what I hoped was an expression of self-deprecating humility and said with a cheerful Southern accent, "Oh no, ma'am, I didn't bring a flat iron with me. All I used this morning was a blow dryer, which I always have to use because my hair is *so* thick!" I may or may not have punctuated the proclamation with a slight head toss.

However, Madame Suzette didn't return my smile. In fact, she seemed a little confused and embarrassed. It wasn't until the young woman she'd sent away on the feminine-hygiene-product errand walked back in the room and sheepishly approached me offering a tampon in one hand and a maxi pad in the other with the exact

. . . .

same question, "Do you use thee long wans or thee short wans?" that I realized what Madame Suzette had actually been referring to. I think the entire female staff at the orphanage is now mentally scarred because they think I use a blow dryer *down there*. Dear Jesus, come quickly!

I've been stretched way beyond my comfort zone a lot lately (and have stretched a few others right along with me). Beyond what I thought the elasticity of my heart and mind—and some days even my reputation—could take. Interestingly enough, it's becoming much more comfortable.

Three days after that most embarrassing moment (let me clarify, that was not my *most* embarrassing moment; more embarrassing is the fact that it barely registered a blip on the radar of dumb things I've ever done), I was returning home to Nashville via the Miami airport when an older woman sitting next to me on the tram asked, "You headed home?" I smiled and said, "Yes, ma'am." She said, "Where you flying to?" I said, "Nashville, Tennessee." Her voice rose with positive affirmation as she responded, "Oh, I *like* Tennessee. I mean, I've never been there myself, but I like what I've seen on TV and stuff. Where you coming from?" I was so tired that I didn't really want to get into a long conversation with a stranger, but she was chatty and seemed lonely, so I explained that I'd been in Haiti all week because I was adopting a little girl with HIV from a village about two hours southwest of Port-au-Prince.

And her demeanor switched from cheerfully inquisitive to thinly disguised disapproval faster than a Georgia boy cracks pecans. She pursed her lips, inhaled slowly, expulsed air forcefully through her nose (which reminded me of an irritated horse), and then announced with an air of frustration, "Me and my husband couldn't have children the *normal* way and a lot of folks told us we should just adopt but I said, 'No, sir!' I mean, I respect what you're doing and all and I hope it works out for you, but it ain't worth all the trouble to me. I mean a lot of them babies die or they grow up and don't even act grateful you took 'em in." She paused for several long seconds in a conversation that had become more awkward than the one with Madame Suzette. Then she repeated softly, "I just don't see how it could be worth all that trouble."

I think her presupposition is the splinter in the thumb of humanity. It's what causes the church to sometimes behave more like a country club than a compassionate community of Christ followers. It's also the muse that prompted me to write this book and wrestle with the following questions:

> *When is it worth being stretched beyond my comfort zone?*
> *When is it worth "overspending" myself for the sake of the gospel?*
> *If I erased all the commitments on my iCal this month, would anybody besides my dentist or the pest control guy really care?*
> *What exactly did Jesus mean when He said, "If you cling to your life, you will lose it; but if you give up your life for me, you will find it."* (Matthew 10:39 NLT)

When my publisher suggested the title *Overextended . . . and Loving Most of It*, I was hesitant. Mainly because I'm a burn-the-candle-at-both-ends kind of girl with lots of room for improvement when it comes to creating margins for rest. My calendar is so often double-booked that I have alerts for my alerts. Buzz after buzz. My purse vibrates so much it looks as if it's being tasered. All too often I live like I believe busyness is a spiritual fruit. So I was concerned that *advertising* being overextended might just prompt God to send a wee lightning bolt my way. Good night, the last thing I want to do is goad people to get busier!

But then I had a conversation with a friend over coffee that convinced me being *overextended* can be biblical. My friend Suzanne has seven children (four biological and three adopted, one of whom has HIV), she co-founded and helps run an international orphan awareness and social justice organization called 147 Million Orphans (which is how I got connected with the little girl I'm in the process of adopting), and she's often understandably frazzled. That particular morning she started laughing when she plopped down next to me with her mocha because she realized she was wearing mismatched socks.

Then, with a huge grin she said, "You know, I think this is what we're supposed to look like when we stand before Jesus. I don't think we're supposed to show up in glory with time to spare, a fresh manicure, and perfect hair. I think if we're really living the gospel, we're going to fall at His feet exhausted and messy, with mismatched socks, just plumb worn out from loving people as hard as we can!"

I thought, *She's right.* Life isn't always orderly and relationships rarely fold neatly with hospital corners. *Real* life . . . *abundant* life . . . *God-honoring* life is about loving Jesus and the people He allows us to rub shoulders with

. . . .

well. Which means some days we'll be stretched emotionally and physically. We'll be taxed to the max. We'll be exhausted. We'll probably even embarrass ourselves in the process. Thankfully, God can expand our hearts, minds, bodies, and calendars to accommodate our calling.

Because loving our Redeemer and loving the world around us *Really. Is. Worth. It.*

I think that was pretty much the point Jesus was making in Luke 10 when he gave a stinker of an attorney a tutorial about expanding his orthopraxy—the way he *lived out* his faith.

> Then an expert on the law stood up to test Jesus, saying, "Teacher, what must I do to get life forever?" Jesus said, "What is written in the law? What do you read there?" The man answered, "Love the Lord your God with all your heart, all your soul, all your strength, and all your mind." Also, "Love your neighbor as you love yourself." Jesus said to him, "Your answer is right. Do this and you will live." But the man, wanting to show the importance of his question, said to Jesus, "And who is my neighbor?" (Luke 10:25–29 NCV)

Evidence this fellow is wisdom-challenged is clear at both the beginning and the end of this passage. First of all, he deigns to call Jesus, "Teacher" (*didaskalos* in Greek[2]) instead of "Lord." It's bad enough this ambulance chaser pops up from his chair to *test* the King of All Kings; you can almost hear the disdain dripping from his question. But worse still, he pointedly addresses Jesus by a common Jewish title used for rabbis instead of a title distinguishing Him as the Messiah, as Immanuel . . . *God With Us*.

He didn't recognize the deity and supremacy of our Savior.

Of course, our Redeemer doesn't get ruffled by the lawyer's slight. He simply turns the table and asks a few questions of His own. And when this well-educated, Perry-Mason-wannabe gives the correct Old Testament answer: *Love the Lord your God with all your heart, all your soul, all your strength, and all your mind. Also, love your neighbor as you love yourself* (Luke 10:27 NCV), Jesus lowers the boom with a simple charge, *Do this and you will live* (Luke 10:28b NCV).

Wow, that's a powerful statement: "Do this and you will *live* [emphasis mine]." At which point I think the haughty barrister should've dropped to his knees on the floor in front of Jesus and said something along these lines:

. . . .

Oh crud, the jig's up! I don't love Jehovah with all my heart, soul, mind and strength! I've tried—believe me I have—but some days I find myself more concerned about the new tax code than the Torah. I want to worship God and live an honorable life but I'm totally inept when it comes to even loving my wife well. So there's obviously no way I can love my neighbors unconditionally. In fact, the ones across the street get on my last nerve because they turn their music up way too loud, they have a beagle that keeps me up half the night with his howling, and I'm pretty sure they're piggybacking on my Wi-Fi account! Please forgive me, Messiah, because I'm a crooked-hearted moron.

But he doesn't confess anything close. Instead, he has the audacity to ask The Alpha and Omega a condescending question, "And just what exactly do you mean by the word *neighbor?*"

This guy *Did. Not. Get. It.* So Jesus lowers the comprehension bar for Mr. Compassion-Challenged and launches into a story:

Jesus answered, "As a man was going down from Jerusalem to Jericho, some robbers attacked him. They tore off his clothes, beat him, and left him lying there, almost dead. It happened that a priest was going down that road. When he saw the man, he walked by on the other side. Next, a Levite came there, and after he went over and looked at the man, he walked by on the other side of the road. (Luke 10:30–32 NCV)

During the time of Christ's earthly ministry, there was only one route from Jerusalem to Jericho, and it was commonly referred to as "The Way of Blood" because of its reputation for criminal activity. It was a treacherous, winding, rocky trail that descended almost 3,500 feet in 17 miles. And what makes Jesus' tale even more interesting is His emphasis that the priest and the Levite were walking down this infamous boulevard *from* Jerusalem *to* Jericho.

Which implies they were likely headed home from their offices at the Temple in the Holy City to their homes in the suburbs of Jericho. The priest had probably been up to his elbows in blood all week, slaughtering sheep for sacrifice. And when he wasn't being a holy butcher, he'd been listening to people pour out their problems. Plus, he'd blessed a boatload of colicky babies. Although Levites were subordinate to priests in Temple hierarchy,[3] surely he too had been working hard all week assisting in the Jewish traditions of worship. He'd burned candles until he didn't have any nose hair left, belted out praise

....

tunes until he was hoarse, and polished the pews until his arms ached. They've both been very *busy* working for Jehovah.

So my guess is they were both pretty jazzed about going to their respective homes to relax. Maybe to watch a little JSPN—the Jerusalem Sports Programming Network—or putter around in the garage, or go fishing. I'm obviously taking a little liberty with the Greek here, but it's important to understand where these two have been and where they're going. It's important because of a ceremonial law which states that anyone who touches a dead body shall be rendered unclean for seven days (Numbers 19:11). Therefore, some people think the priest and the Levite didn't stop to help the guy in the gully because he appeared near death and they were afraid of breaking that rule.

However, the fact that Jesus says they were walking *away* from Jerusalem and *toward* Jericho makes that a moot point. Whatever ritual purity they may have been protecting because of their responsibilities in the Temple didn't matter much if they were headed home. They didn't have to worry about being ceremonially unclean because they weren't going to have to perform ceremonies in the suburbs. Now let me digress by saying these two fellas might well have been nice guys. Obviously they were loyal and dutiful if they were on the Temple's payroll. They probably coached Little League and maybe even mowed the lawn of a single mom in their cul-de-sac.

Jesus doesn't necessarily paint them unneighborly. He simply explains they didn't recognize the scope of *His neighborhood*. They missed the privilege of stretching beyond the confines of their calendars and job descriptions to pour grace on someone who was desperate for it. Fortunately, the Samaritan had wiped enough fog off his relational glasses to understand that *anyone* Jehovah allowed him to rub shoulders with was a neighbor.

> Then a Samaritan traveling down the road came to where the hurt man was. When he saw the man, he felt very sorry for him. The Samaritan went to him, poured olive oil and wine on his wounds, and bandaged them. Then he put the hurt man on his own donkey and took him to an inn where he cared for him. The next day, the Samaritan brought out two coins, gave them to the innkeeper, and said, "Take care of this man. If you spend more money on him, I will pay it back to you when I come again." (Luke 10:33–35 NCV)

By now Jesus' story had the poor attorney's boxers all bunched up because not only had He exposed the pettiness of his silly "neighbor" question, but now Jesus was also portraying a trashy Samaritan as the star of the parable. The barrister was probably thinking, *Oh good night, I need to escape from this train wreck of a conversation before the inmates take over the asylum!* Remember, during this period of ancient history most Jews despised Samaritans. They despised them because the Samaritan race—who were often the offspring of one Assyrian parent and one Jewish parent—were a reminder of Assyria's invasion and dominance over Israel.

Therefore, an observant Jewish person considered a Samaritan's existence something that threatened, diluted, and polluted the purity of the Jewish race. And the tension between the two reached an impasse after the Jewish remnant repatriated back to Jerusalem following the Babylonian captivity (approximately 750 BC) because that's when they refused the Samaritan's offer to help them rebuild the Temple.[4]

Basically, this is how the Jewish settlers responded to the well-meaning Samaritans: *Mind your own business, you bunch of dirty half-breeds. We'd rather starve than take your filthy money!* So the Samaritans stormed off in a rebuffed huff and built their own temple on top of Mount Gerizim, complete with their own version of the priesthood, essentially desecrating everything the Jews held sacred.

In a modern context, being a Samaritan living near Israel during the first century would be like being the child of a white mama and a black daddy and living in the American Deep South in the 1950s and early '60s. Suffice it to say, the Hatfields and the McCoys were BFFs compared to the Jews and the Samaritans.

And to add even more color to the conversation Christ was having with this out-of-his-league attorney, just one chapter earlier in Luke, an entire Samaritan village had rejected Jesus Himself (Luke 9:51–56). This made James and John so mad they asked Jesus if they could call down fire from heaven and fry the Samaritans into oblivion (which also gives us a little insight into why Jesus nicknamed James and John the "Sons of Thunder" in Mark 3:17).

Now, in light of all this history, you would think that Jesus—being a Jew—would've made the Samaritan the bad guy in this story. Or at the very least, the guy in the ditch—the one who needed help. Instead, He makes him the hero. And then He encourages the attorney to stretch the boundaries of his heart and mind to model unreserved kindness too:

> Then Jesus said, "Which one of these three men do you think was a neighbor to the man who was attacked by the robbers?" The expert on the law answered, "The one who showed him mercy." Jesus said to him, "Then go and do what he did." (Luke 10:36–37 NCV)

....

The story of the Good Samaritan underscores a running theme in the Bible: *people matter to God*. And He expects them to matter to us as well. Additionally, this familiar parable highlights a principle that God has been pounding into my hard head a lot over the past few years: *part of the blessing is in the stretch itself.* In other words, when compassion is coupled with inconvenience, it's sweeter. Because if I only extend kindness when it's convenient or natural for me, then I don't need much of God's help to make the investment. But when I give from an account that already feels overdrawn, then I *have* to depend on Him to transform my meager capacity into grace that benefits the receiver!

I got home from teaching at a conference in Atlanta late one night recently, went to bed, and was tossing and turning (due to my middle-aged-chick hormone fluctuations). The following morning I hit the snooze button twice before groaning out of bed to get ready for church. Worship was awesome, yet I couldn't help but be a tad distracted because the deadline for this book was in fourteen days and I still had a long ways to go. About forty thousand words of a long ways. That's about the equivalent of typing day and night until it's due in my publisher's in-box.

Writing the bulk of a book in two weeks wouldn't normally pose much of a problem because I'm a fast typist and have already completed most of the research for this project. Plus, my friend Sheila gave me a darling, candy-apple-red espresso machine for Christmas and the go-go juice it spews keeps me alert for ten hours at a stretch.

However, my adoption dossier had just been approved in Haiti a few days prior to the event in Atlanta (making it necessary for me to fly to Haiti immediately to visit the US Embassy, Haitian Immigration, and my agency in Port-au-Prince, all this past week), which cut my writing time in half. Mind you, I was willing to *walk* to Miami and *swim* to Haiti in order to get my little girl, so I didn't begrudge flying there. It's just that this traveling part in the adoption process couldn't have come at a more inconvenient time vocationally. Basically, I had my own "baby in a ditch" to deal with while business went on at its usual frenetic pace.

By the time our church service was ending, I was acutely aware of the need to buckle down and type until my fingers cramped, so I drove straight home, opened my laptop, and got to work. Right about the time I imagined smoke was about to waft from the keyboard, I decided to take a break and go for a quick trail run with the more athletic of my two dogs, Cookie.

I threw on a fleece over my T-shirt, laced up a pair of Nikes, and encouraged Cookie to hustle into the car in an effort to be as time-efficient as possible. She and I were racing up a trail at the Natchez Trace wilderness area within fifteen minutes, though I was panting noticeably harder than Cookie. I chose the two-mile route instead of the five-mile path—assuring my furry, straining-against-the-leash companion that we'd have time for long runs in the future. Exactly 18:39 later we came barreling back out to the trailhead, finished with our jaunt.

And that's when I spotted a scruffy-looking guy in the picnic shelter next to the parking lot. He was tinkering with an old bicycle, which was so loaded down with threadbare commuter bags it looked more like a barge. Based on the heft of his vehicle and the wildness of his beard, it looked like he'd been pedaling for quite awhile. Cookie and I trotted over, introduced ourselves, and found out his name is Jason and he was nearing the end of an incredible 605-mile journey from New Orleans to Cookeville, Tennessee!

He seemed a little embarrassed by the attention, so I only conversed with him a few minutes and then walked back to my car, pondering how the expression in his eyes seemed tired and wounded. I considered what might possibly compel someone to ride an ancient bike from the bayous of Louisiana to the hills of Tennessee. I wondered if he was running from something. Or someone.

Because that Sunday was the first warm, sunny day in

quite some time, I rolled down the windows and opened the sunroof on the way home. As the wind shifted papers around in the backseat, the Holy Spirit shifted something in me too. He nudged me from efficiency toward compassion. He prompted me to go and get some money from my wallet at home (I didn't have any cash with me, only my driver's license) and take it back to Jason. At first I thought, *Well, shoot a monkey! I've already spent time I didn't have to spare to go for a run and that's going to take at least another twenty or thirty minutes.* But then I sensed the Spirit whisper firmly, "People are always more important than projects, Lisa." And I replied sheepishly, "Yes, sir" to the wind.

I'm so very glad I did.

After going home and grabbing a few bills from my wallet, I drove back to the Natchez Trace, all the while rehearsing a conversational disclaimer in my mind so as not to alarm the skittish biker when I approached him a second time. I thought I'd say something like, *Please forgive me if this comes across as presumptuous. I certainly don't want to offend you, but God impressed me to share this with you if that's okay.* However, when I pulled up, Jason wasn't where I'd left him. His camel of a bicycle was, though, and the wrench and screwdriver he'd been using were now sitting on a picnic table next to it. It was obvious he'd just stepped away for a minute or two.

....

So I walked back to the car, grabbed a notepad from the glove compartment, and wrote "Love, God" in big letters and "P.S. I haven't forgotten you" below that and folded the sheet of paper around the cash. Then I walked over to the trail, picked up a pretty stone, and placed it on top of the love note right beside Jason's tools where he'd be sure to notice it. I drove away smiling, hoping it would be a happy surprise when that weary traveler unwrapped a small, unexpected gift reminding him that the Creator of the Universe cared about him. Imagining his moment of discovery was infinitely more valuable than the thirty minutes of diversion it took.

Now I'm feeling energized and I'm actually looking forward to the next stretch of writing . . . even if it's *a long wan*.

2

MIDDLE-AGED STRETCH MARKS

I used to be afraid of failing at something that
really mattered to me, but now I'm more afraid
of succeeding at things that don't matter.[1]

—*Bob Goff*

Octber 2011 marks the beginning of the biggest
overextension of my life thus far, which was
when I dove headfirst into the tumultuous sea
of adoption. I'd been pondering adoption for years. Well,
for decades, actually. You see, Cindy Whelchel—my best
friend in high school—and I had made a pact when we
were seventeen that we were going to adopt babies no one

else wanted and we hoped we'd win the lottery of adoption and get brown babies. We're both white but prefer black culture, abhor racial prejudice, and—truth be told—we were probably hoping that having mocha-colored kids would give us the opportunity to talk back in church!

Of course, we had no idea when we made that solemn promise, while wearing matching pink Izods and sporting pouffy hair in the eighties, that Cindy would marry Peter in the nineties and then struggle with infertility and go on to adopt two precious children (who just so happen to be biracial). Nor did we imagine that, thirty years later, in 2012, I'd still be single (I often tease and say my husband is lost and won't stop to ask for directions).

Frankly, being unmarried is the main reason I pondered adoption for so long but never seriously pursued it. I grew up in the Waltons and Huxtables era, so the idea of having a child without a dad was pretty foreign to me. But when an old friend called last year and asked if I'd be willing to adopt a hardcore crack addict's baby that no one else was standing in line for (because of the inevitable neurological problems and possible birth defects), I thought, *This soon-to-be mama and the baby she's carrying need someone—anyone—to love them, and even an older girl with chemically dependent hair like me can do that!*

And so began a roller-coaster ride doing life alongside a precious young woman who sold her petite, scarred body to a steady stream of men for ten or twenty dollars per encounter . . . just enough cash to score another hit. "Marie" was rarely coherent enough to care about what the drugs were doing to the baby girl growing inside her belly. She was little more than a child herself mentally, but every now and then her eyes would focus and she would listen intently when I told her she was worth *So. Much. More* than the way she was currently living. In those rare moments of clarity, she would let me throw away her crack pipe and would promise to go to the rehab facility we found that was willing to take her in.

The following journal entries (which my friend Jenny posted on Facebook and Twitter to establish an ongoing prayer team) reveal why I now have permanent stretch marks on my heart, as well as my hips—even though I've never actually carried a child in my body!

December 29, 2011

Dear Friends, Facebook buddies and Twitter peeps,

I need your help. Some of you know I'm in the process of adopting the baby girl of a precious young woman named Marie (that's not exactly her name because I want to protect her privacy), who's also a hardcore crack cocaine

. . . .

addict. Unfortunately, Marie is having a very hard time staying clean, is refusing to go to rehab at this point and, according to the OB-GYN who examined her a few days ago, will lose the baby she's carrying unless she stops smoking crack and makes it to the thirty-six week mark of her pregnancy, which is nine weeks away.

So I'm asking everyone I know (or almost know via the Internet) to join me in a prayer campaign called "Marie Mondays," to fight for the life of both Marie and her unborn child who I'm hoping to become the mama of. If God impresses you to join me on this journey, I'll be sending out a new verse each week for us to intentionally pray together, as well as updates on both Marie and the baby. I'm also asking for you to prayerfully consider fasting one meal—or even one cup of coffee if you're a caffeine lover like me!—every Monday in a collab-orative appeal for Jesus to marshal an army of His angels to form a supernatural "wall" that will keep the baby safe in the womb until the time is right for her to be born.

Finally, if/when you have a few spare moments, I'd really appreciate it if you'd write Marie a note encouraging her to lean into the unconditional love of God (she delights in getting mail and was thrilled when I told her some of my friends might be sending her cards and letters). Marie had the most horrifically abusive childhood imaginable, was in foster care for a long time, has multiple mental and emotional problems, and as a result doesn't think she's worth loving. But I believe God is beginning to change her negative perspective about herself and I believe real healing and restoration is possible.

"Marie mail" can be sent to:

(a crisis pregnancy center in Central Florida handled the correspondence)

The expression "thank you" falls far short of the gratitude I have for your help. But until some brilliant wordsmith comes up with a better phrase, thank you . . . from the bottom of my heart!

Lisa Harper

P.S. The verses we're praying this week are from Psalm 147:5-6: Our Lord is great, vast in power. His understanding is infinite. The LORD helps the afflicted but brings the wicked to the ground" (HSCB).

"Father, please help Marie, as she is truly the most afflicted of your sheep I know. Please calm the

....

chaos in her heart and mind with Your perfect peace. And please keep the baby safe. Only You have the power to protect them both. Thank You for being slow to anger and rich in compassion. I love and trust You and ask these things in the power and authority of the name of Jesus, Your Son and our Redeemer. Amen."

January 2, 2012

Dear Friends, Prayer Warriors and Warriorettes,

The past week with Marie has been more sad than sweet. She disappeared on a two-day drug binge and has been using steadily since she came back. However, there was a moment of pure grace that took place in the midst of the chaos, not unlike a rose growing out of cement.

Since I live several states away and can only be with Marie every couple of weeks, my mom and two of my aunts have committed to help Andrea (the director of the Crisis Pregnancy Center and an old and dear friend who connected me with Marie, and is basically "command central" of this mission of mercy) by visiting Marie and bringing her food a few times a week.

....

Now my mother is a very petite, very conservative woman who doesn't make a habit of hanging out in crack houses like I do, so this is a stretch for her. But on Friday (Dec. 30th), my Aunt Susan called me and described a scene I will forever treasure: my tiny mama marching confidently up to an intimidating man who was standing outside of the somewhat scary place where Marie stays and announcing kindly yet firmly, "I'm Patti, Lisa's mother, and I'm here to see Marie. I've brought her something to eat."

Susan said he seemed a bit surprised but replied quickly, "Okay, I'll go get her," and sure enough Marie came walking out sheepishly a minute later and headed straight into my mom's outstretched arms (she knows mom because mom spent the day with us at the hospital the week before).

Mom held on to her for a long time, stroking Marie's hair back from her face, kissing her forehead and speaking words of encouragement over her. Then, much to Marie's delight—who's also tiny but eats like a horse—mom gave her two bags filled to the brim with her favorite food.

I was crying so hard after Susan's phone call that I had to pull off the road into a parking

....

lot because I couldn't see! I was—and still am—undone that my precious mother would travel so far outside of her comfort zone simply because she loves Jesus and she loves me.

I hope to have that same kind of brave, tenacious, no-holds-barred love for my little girl, Anna Price (I'm naming her after my sister Theresa, whose middle name is "Anne," my brother John, whose middle name is "Price," and Anna in Luke 2, who never gave up hope that she would literally see Immanuel). Which is still only a thimbleful compared to the vast ocean—of affection our Savior has for each one of us.

Thank you again from the bottom of my heart for your prayers for Marie to stop smoking crack and for Anna Price's safety in her womb. And for your cards and letters, which strengthen Marie's wobbly heart along with mine.

Twenty-seven and a half weeks down and only eight and a half to go!

Gratefully,
Lisa

Verse of the Week: "Real religion, the kind that passes muster before God the Father, is this:

....

Reach out to the homeless and loveless in their plight, and guard against corruption from the godless world." (James 1:27 MSG)

January 9, 2012

Dear Social Media Fellow Sojourners,

It's been another hard week with Marie; she continues to smoke crack on a daily basis and stayed out all night partying several times. Thankfully, because of the miraculous grace of God, she and the baby have made it another seven days. Which means Anna Price only has seven and a half more weeks before she can be born.

Seven and a half weeks: less time than a grading period in school; less time than the summer season we enjoy between July the Fourth and Labor Day; less time than most movies stay in theaters; less time than it usually takes me to lose ten pounds. Yet today, seven and a half weeks feels like forever. I find myself sitting here before our Redeemer silently . . . with no coherent words to pray. I'm simply clinging to the truth that He is merciful and His purposes are always for our good and His glory. And I'm choosing to believe

. . . .

that means less than two months from now I'll be holding a tiny warrior of a daughter.

The most positive thing that happened this week is the man Marie lives with got arrested. Therefore, it will be more difficult for her to get money for drugs (he basically financed her habit). Unfortunately, she's already turned to other guys for money—to exploitive predators who aren't remotely interested in what's best for her. One of them snuck out the back door when Andrea went by to visit Marie this afternoon, which of course made me feel like sending my little brother over with a BB gun!

But I realize the only truly effective ammunition in this battle is prayer. And the most powerful plea I've heard lately came from the lips of my dear friend Judy's ten-year-old daughter, Katie, who bowed her head before dinner last night and said: "Dear Jesus, please keep Marie and the baby safe."

Thank you very, very much for your continued commitment to bring that same request to our Heavenly Father.

Gratefully,

Lisa

....

Verses of the Week: "The Lord lifts the poor from the dirt and takes the helpless from the ashes. He seats them with princes, the princes of his people. He gives children to the woman who has none and makes her a happy mother. Praise the Lord!" (Psalm 113:7–9 NCV)

January 16, 2012

This "Marie Monday" update is later than usual because I had two days off and was able to fly to Florida to be with Marie yesterday and today. Therefore, I wanted to write this note after our visit (we hugged goodbye about an hour ago) so the news would be as current as possible. I'm now sitting in the Orlando airport waiting to board the flight to Nashville. I'm exhausted, hopeful, overwhelmed, sad, and absolutely desperate for God's strength and guidance after spending the last twenty-four hours near Marie. Loving a hardcore addict is the hardest calling I've ever said "yes" to and to say I'm in over my head is an understatement.

It always feels surreal to transition back to normalcy after I've been with Marie. To see people in the gate area nonchalantly sipping Starbucks

....

or reading *USA Today* with Micky Mouse ears perched crookedly on their balding heads. It's hard to believe that just last night Andrea and I were slumped in filthy lawn chairs in front of Marie's residence, giggling uncontrollably over the absurdity that we—two conservative, Jesus-loving nerds—had basically become the Christian version of Cagney and Lacey! Of course, that was after we'd had our hearts pummeled by the harsh reality of caring for Marie (who was high as a kite on crack) and dealing with the "dates" she'd made with men who give her money in exchange for sexual favors so that she can buy more drugs.

Many of you have asked why she hasn't been arrested and the answer is complicated. I can tell you there are several compassionate police officers and sheriff's deputies who are actively involved and doing everything they can. Unfortunately, we're discovering the system is so geared toward protecting people's civil rights that a young, mentally impaired, pregnant addict can very easily slip between the cracks. And Anna Price has "zero rights" to governmental protection until she's born, according to a ten-der-hearted deputy who was just itching to help

....

but said his hands were "as cuffed as a convicted criminal" in a situation like this.

The good news is that Marie was clean for at least four hours today so she and Anna Price had a brief reprieve from the crack monster. We went to a small lake and fed the ducks, wandered around a Martin Luther King festival, went for a walk beside a big lake and scanned the bumpy surface for alligators, and then ate lunch at Red Lobster—which wouldn't be my first choice but because their shrimp fettucini alfredo makes Marie's face light up like a Christmas tree, that's where we went. And frankly, now every time I see a Red Lobster sign my heart leaps because their food has nourished my unborn daughter more than any other chain restaurant. I'll probably buy stock at some point!

Thank you, thank you, thank you for choosing to pray with us and for us. Marie and Anna Price have become so precious to me . . . I cannot imagine life without them. And I am convinced that God's compassion—illuminated through the prayers of His people—is what is keeping them both alive. Only six and a half weeks to go.

Gratefully,

Lisa

. . . .

Verses of the Week: "Jesus traveled through all the towns and villages, teaching in their synagogues, preaching the Good News about the kingdom, and healing all kinds of diseases and sicknesses. When he saw the crowds, he felt sorry for them because they were hurting and helpless, like sheep without a shepherd." (Matthew 9:35–36 NCV)

January 23, 2012

Dear Marie Monday Family,

This past Wednesday night during our small group time at The Next Door (which is a six-month, residential recovery program for women with alcohol and drug dependency issues), I noticed some of my girls were wide–eyed and seemed flustered while I was gabbing on enthusiastically about Jesus. Although my mouth kept running, my mind paused and wondered: *Have I said something shocking or confusing or inappropriate?* It wasn't until one of them graciously interrupted me and said, "Lisa, your shirt's busted," that I looked down and saw the zipper on my hoodie had split apart, completely

....

exposing me from neck to waist. Talk about letting it all hang out in Bible study!

I knew when I began writing these "Marie Monday" updates about my adoption journey it was going to be a revealing experience. I knew I was essentially putting my heart on a public shelf. But I believed—still do—that the price of exposure was worth the payoff of recruiting an army of prayer warriors to fight for God's will to be accomplished. Frankly, I'd be willing to post my actual weight on Twitter or Facebook if it meant a tribe of believers would then beseech our Creator-Redeemer to turn Marie away from crack cocaine and back toward Him, as well as to keep Anna Price safe in her womb until the time is right for her to be born! Thankfully, most of you have done just that for several weeks, for which I will be forever grateful, regardless of what unfolds during the next month and a half.

There are, however, a few people who have questioned my motives regarding Marie and her unborn baby. And while I know it's foolish to respond to every detractor in an open forum, I would like to clarify a few things in light of the seriousness of this situation.

First of all, I'm a sinner with a crooked heart.

....

Apart from the correction and direction of the Holy Spirit, I'm prone to being a selfish stinker. So I spent a lot of time in prayer and Christian counseling before even sticking my toe into the adoption pool. And I've continued to get professional and pastoral counseling throughout this process. It has taken many, many years for God to prepare me for motherhood (not that anyone is ever truly prepared for what has to be the most wonderful, difficult, joyful, heart-wrenching miracle this side of glory), and I feel especially called to care for a child who isn't wanted or whose biological parent(s) cannot take care of her.

Furthermore, my desire is for both Marie and Anna Price to be as healthy as possible. For Marie, that means to stop smoking crack; for the baby, that means being born. These are the two goals— two lives actually—we are praying for and working toward. Unfortunately, Marie is still unwilling to go to rehab or give up the addictive lifestyle she's been entrenched in for many years. That doesn't mean we've given up hope on her restoration, it just means we recognize that no human has the power to rescue her or mend all that's broken in her life.

But Andrea and I are committed to keep loving her—more importantly, to keep explaining how much God loves her. And we'll keep trying to help her realize that she's worth SO. MUCH. MORE than the way she's living. We'll also continue to make sure she has plenty of food to eat. And Andrea will keep coaxing her out of bed when she's high and combative and somehow get her into the car and drive her to all of her medical appointments—just like she's been doing freely and compassionately for women in crisis pregnancies for more than a decade. We will not stop caring for Marie and we will never, ever view her as a "baby factory." She is a precious, limping lamb of God, who deserves to be loved and healed.

I hope this update helps clarify the motives of my heart and allays legitimate concern. However, I will be grieved if it prompts anyone to rally to my defense. Please do not send tweets or FB messages about what a "good person" I am. I am not a good person nor am I on some heroic quest. I am a messy, mistake-prone woman who's been lavished with divine grace and feels called to parent; to do what millions of people—what most of you—do beautifully and brokenly every day for your children. If God fulfills my dream of becoming someone's mama, it will be yet another tangible example of His overwhelming kindness.

....

Finally, please accept my deepest appreciation for your ongoing prayers and for your letters to Marie. I have to believe heaven is responding because, against all odds, Anna Price is still kicking like a champion soccer player in utero and is almost three pounds! Praise be to our God alone!

Warmest Regards,
Lisa

Verses for the Week: "The king is not saved by his great army; a warrior is not delivered by his great strength. The war horse is a false hope for salvation, and by its great might it cannot rescue. Behold the eye of the LORD is on those who fear him, on those who hope in his steadfast love, that he may deliver their soul from death and keep them alive in famine. Our soul waits for the LORD; he is our help and our shield." (Psalm 33:16–20)

January 30, 2012

Dear, dear Friends,

This past week was pretty crazy: I was at a conference in Alabama for two days, then had

....

meetings in Dallas for three days, was in Nashville (home) for one day, and then was off to Denver and Nebraska for three days. (Where I got to pray with forty women who put their hope in Jesus for the first time, which was awesome!) In the middle of this whirling dervish week, my dear friend Sheila asked me a gentle, poignant question: How are you able to focus on anything else right now in light of everything that's going on with Marie and the baby?

I told her my mind never wanders very far from Marie and Anna Price. I find myself often wondering if Marie's inhaling from a crack pipe at that particular moment; I wonder if she's eating every time I sit down to a meal; when I'm in the car, I wonder if she's safe inside or if she's walking barefoot next to a busy highway (as she's prone to do, especially when she's high or on the hunt for more drugs). And of course, I wonder whether the baby's still moving in her tummy. If Anna Price's tiny heart is still beating like a loud drum. If she's still kicking like a champion soccer player. If she's still fighting to gulp "fresh air" in spite of all the toxins that assault her daily in the womb.

Through it all, God has been teaching me to walk behind Him. To remember that He's the one with the big sword. That He's the only one who's able to slay the nasty dragons of hardcore addiction, prostitution, and shame. I find myself regularly running to Jesus for perseverance and hope and faith because I've used all mine up. And I've learned that I can't ride every single wave in Marie's ocean. There are good swells, like when she's clear-headed and talks sweetly about how one day the three of us—her, Anna Price, and me—can go to the beach together. Or when she tells Andrea that she'd like to start going to church.

But there are lots of heart-crushing break-ers, like when Marie disappears on a drug binge and we can't find her for days at a time. Or when she yells at Andrea with words that would make a sailor wince. Or when she claps her hands, giddy about the sixty dollars she's about to make by having sex with one of her "customers" because that money will pay for six small crack rocks.

I have to rest in God's sovereign mercy in order to keep risking my heart. I have to keep walking behind the Lord. Even then, all I can do is the Next. Right. Thing. So the adoption paperwork is final-ized. My home study is complete. Pediatricians who specialize in babies born to addicted mamas have been consulted. I'm currently reading a book on infant massage (crack babies are notoriously hard to soothe). I've lined up lots of friends and family members who've committed to take turns holding and comforting Anna Price for the first few weeks after she's born, if I get to keep her. And along with so many of you, I keep praying.

Three pounds. Healthy Lungs. Strong Heart. Only four or five weeks to go.

Thank you from the bottom of my heart,

Lisa

Verse of the Week: "They will have no fear of bad news; their hearts are steadfast, trusting in the LORD." (Psalm 112:7 NIV)

February 6, 2012

Dear Fellow Wobbly-Yet-Hopeful Sheep,

We only have three and a half weeks until Anna Price can be born and I'm beyond grateful that God has kept her and Marie safe thus far. Against unbelievable odds, they both passed their last doctor's exam on Thursday with flying colors and I truly believe your prayers have been the most

. . . .

effective factor in their well-being. So please keep petitioning our Heavenly Father on their behalf . . . please pray that Anna Price will continue to kick like a soccer star and that Marie will quit smoking crack for good and find restoration in the healing arms of Jesus. It's beginning to look like a miracle really might happen with the birth of this precious baby girl!

However, as many of you know, the adoption process doesn't follow a straight line and is extremely unpredictable. In my particular experience, it's been like playing that whack-a-mole game at Chucky Cheese. Because it seems like every time we get one problem solved, another even bigger one surfaces. Therefore, to make a long story short, I won't know if I get to be Anna Price's mama until forty-eight hours after she's born. And if that happens, it will be miracle #2. Well actually, miracle #3, because miracle #1 will be for Anna Price to have life outside the womb and miracle #2 will be Marie's recovery. And the miracles really are in that sequence in my mind.

That's not to say I've stopped hoping to bring Anna Price home to Tennessee, because I do. More than I've ever hoped for anything in this world. But frankly, hanging on to hope through

. . . .

the ups and downs of this situation has worn me down to the dregs of myself. I'm exhausted from dealing with the effects of drug abuse and prostitution and mental instability and emotional chaos and the realities of human suffering. I don't think I can last much longer than three or four more weeks! Yet through it all, God keeps propping up my wilting, oh-so-imperfect self and reminding me that He REALLY. IS. IN. CONTROL. That whatever happens, He will ultimately work all of this out for good. Because He is a perfectly faithful and compassionate Redeemer.

So in this moment, on this Marie Monday, it's enough that Anna Price and Marie are alive and that Marie went to church with her boyfriend yesterday for the first time in years!

Thank you again—from the bottom of my raggedy heart—for sacrificing your time to pray for us.

Lisa

Verses for the Week: "Fig trees may not grow figs, and there may be no grapes on the vines. There may be no olives growing and no food growing in the fields. There may be no sheep in the pens

. . . .

and no cattle in the barns. But I will still be glad in the LORD; I will rejoice in God my Savior. The Lord GOD is my strength. He makes me like a deer that does not stumble so I can walk on the steep mountains." (Habakkuk 3:17–19 NCV)

At this point in my extremely stretching adoption voyage, my hands were wrapped around the gunwales of the boat with a white-knuckled grip, but I could see the promised land of parenthood on the horizon, just a mere month away. And so I held on for dear life and hoped.

3

TAKING THE AGNES CHALLENGE

Vulnerability is not knowing victory or
defeat, it's understanding the necessity of
both; it's engaging. It's being all in.[1]

— *Brené Brown*

absolutely love talking to people about Jesus at conferences around the country, but I don't absolutely love the
getting there and coming home part. The planes, trains,
hotels, cabs, and church vans part. Last year I was on
the road more days than I was home in Tennessee. And I

know some people romanticize about traveling for a living and assume it's a cushy existence softened by Egyptian cotton sheets, room service, and marble bathrooms you don't have to clean yourself; but that isn't usually my experience.

A few weeks ago, my hotel room came with a human-hairs-that-weren't-mine-in-the-bed bonus, along with a cigarette-butt surprise in the commode. On the trip prior to that, an anxious woman who'd never driven to the airport by herself before was assigned the task of carting me to and from said airport. Of course, she took the wrong toll road on the way there. Twice. I had to run down the concourse to make my flight—which isn't all that unusual but is getting harder as the years roll by because of the extra fluff I've accumulated from eating the lumberjack portions served by most restaurants on the road.

Then there was the time a few months ago that I spent six hours in an airport on the way home from an event because the flight to Nashville kept getting delayed. After the first delay, the brand new gate agent got so flustered by travelers' questions regarding whether or not they were going to miss their connecting flights that she literally ran away from the gate area in tears. This subsequently branded all of my fellow passengers and me as trouble-makers (mind you, only three or four people had asked her questions because Nashville was the final destination for most of us, so we didn't have to worry about connecting flights) based on the frowning, bossy bully who replaced her an hour later.

After a stern reprimand during which he instructed us not to ask him *One. Single. Question.* regarding our flight's departure time, he gave us the silent treatment for a few hours. Then he gleefully announced our flight was canceled. Of course, there were no other flights to Nashville that evening *and* the airline refused to off-load our luggage. So we hiked to the shuttle pick-up area approximately seven miles away, waited for our midnight ride for about twenty minutes in the snow, and then were unceremoniously dropped off at a very low-budget hotel that I'm pretty sure rented rooms by the hour based on the clientele I noticed at the Waffle House next door while waiting in line to check in.

Oh, and they only had smoking rooms left by the time I made it to the front of the line. (I won't tell you what particular airport this travesty took place in because I don't like defaming American industry, but it rhymes with *Schmictroit*. And I won't tell you which particular airline had such fragile and grumpy employees because in my experience most gate agents are lovely individuals, but it rhymes with *Schmelta*.)

Sigh. Suffice it to say, sometimes I'm a less-than-enthusiastic traveler. Sometimes I sort of "bow up" before boarding a plane like I'm getting ready for battle. (In my own defense, I have had to joust many a hairy arms because male frequent flyers seem to be imbued with the sense that *both* armrests belong to them.) I've become adept at using my computer bag as a shield against other passengers' out-of-control carry-ons, and whatever book or newspaper I'm reading as a kind of literary flak jacket to discourage gabby seatmates. Big Bluetooth headphones complete my commuter-combat ensemble and safely seal me into a cocoon of silence.

I was wearing those archetypal "fatigues" recently on a petite plane departing Grand Rapids for Chicago (November 6, 2012). I'd just gotten situated into a kiddie-sized aisle seat and was trying to figure out which knee I wanted to nibble on first when I looked up and noticed an elderly woman loaded with bags (I'm not sure how she got past the gate agent because she definitely had more than two) boarding our motorized aluminum can. With jaded resignation, I thought to myself, *I bet she sits next to me*, because even from twenty-five feet I could tell she was a talker.

Sure enough, after accidentally whacking me upside the head with her purse, she scrambled into the postage-stamp-sized space on my right. I gave her a very brief smile, then pointedly turned my attention back to the book I was reading so as to discourage her from trying to engage me in conversation. Three to five seconds later she chirped, "Are you from Grand Rapids?" It was all I could do not to groan. But I summoned the last shred of decency left in my raggedy self and managed a quick, "No, ma'am." I didn't say where I was from and I didn't return her polite query, hoping she'd take the hint and look out the window or something (my mama would've spanked me if she'd been onboard). Instead, she asked brightly, "Are you from Chicago?" And I thought, *If I wasn't a Bible teacher, I would so order an adult beverage on this flight.*

After a few more kind questions on her part, followed by curt responses on mine, she fell silent. I felt a twinge of guilt for shutting grandma down. But before that guilt led me to repentance, I fell fast asleep on my seatback tray table. Sometime later, though, my iPod must've slid off, because I jerked awake when she tried to gently place it back next to my snoring face. And when I read the concern for me—a sleepy, unresponsive stranger—on her countenance, the seed of my earlier guilt blossomed into a mighty oak tree.

I sheepishly wiped the drool off my cheek and confessed, "I'm sorry I haven't been very friendly so far. I've just had a really hard week and I'm pretty tired. My name is Lisa, what's yours?" To which she smiled broadly and replied, "My name is Agnes and I'm eighty-three years old!" When she told me she was from Grand Rapids, I asked if she was going to Chicago to visit family and it was as if I'd opened the door to Santa's secret toy room. She turned in her seat so that she could face me fully, arched her eyebrows with a sort of mischievous joy and announced, "I'm just flying *through* Chicago, dear—I'm *going* to MUMBAI, INDIA!"

I leaned closer toward her with unmasked curiosity now—totally taken aback that this eighty-three-year-old woman was traveling halfway across the world by herself—and said, "Wow! Why are you going to India, Agnes?" And the happy cat came flying out of the bag when Agnes exclaimed eagerly, "I'm going to India to tell people about *JESUS!*" At which point I thought, *I'm going to be hit by a LIGHTNING BOLT!*

Dear Agnes and I spent the last twenty minutes of the flight gabbing about how good God is. She told me she fell in love with her husband, Jim, when she was fifteen and he was seventeen. They got married two years later, right after she graduated from high school. She had her first baby when she was nineteen years old and soon after that, she put her hope in Jesus Christ and began attending church faithfully. She also began praying that her husband would put his hope in the unconditional love of Christ too. Several years later he did and a few years after that he told Agnes he felt like God was calling him to preach. Of course, God had already disclosed that to her, so she was just waiting for Jim to get the wax out of his ears!

They started a church in Michigan, which began growing like a weed, as did their family after Agnes gave birth to twin boys. She said their life was blessed beyond her wildest dreams until they were in their mid-forties and Jim died unexpectedly. Soon after that, one of her twin sons—who was physically disabled—died. Agnes said she thought her life was over. That she couldn't go on without the love of her life and her son. But she said before she could "really get to wallowing" God spoke to her. He essentially said, "Agnes, I'm the *love* of your life and Jim would want you to *get on with your life!*"

So she picked herself up, dusted herself off, and decided to invest what was left of her life into missions. With a twinkle in her eye she continued, "Lisa, I've been on fifty-one trips outside the US since then and I've never been more content in my life. I've prayed with children in Africa and slept in a hut with a pastor's family in Mongolia. I've had the privilege of traveling all over the world to tell people about Jesus!" I may or may not have fidgeted in that moment, expecting to feel at least a small zap from the lightning bolt I was now convinced God *should* hurl my way.

Right before our wheels hit the tarmac, she lowered her voice and asked almost apologetically, "Will you

....

please remember to pray for me while I'm in India?" I told Agnes I'd be honored to pray for her and then said, "Agnes, I'd also like to pray for you right now if that's okay with you?" She replied, "Oh honey, I'd love that!" When I put one hand on her shoulder and clasped one of her soft, capable hands with my other, I got really tickled because the sudden silence on our plane signaled that the other twenty or so passengers were straining to eavesdrop on our prayer. Then when we deplaned a few minutes later, several of them paused to hug us and promised to pray for Agnes too!

After helping Agnes figure out where she needed to go in O'Hare to catch her next flight to London, I had to race down two concourses to catch mine home to Nashville. But I grinned the whole way, thinking, *I want to be more like Agnes when I grow up!* Meeting Agnes reminded me that another challenging aspect of Christ's conversation with that knot-head of a lawyer in Luke 10 is the word *all*. Love the Lord your God with *all* your heart, *all* your soul, *all* your strength, and *all* your mind.

I want to be *all in* like her when it comes to telling people how much Jesus loves them. I want to be willing to sit in a middle seat all the way to Mumbai. I want to hike up mountains when I'm an octogenarian because there are people who need hugging at the top. I want to be more excited about sharing the gospel when I'm

....

eighty-three than I am now at forty-nine. I want to live a pedal-to-the-metal, no-holds-barred, running-full-tilt-toward-the-throne kind of life.

When it comes to being all in for the sake of the gospel, I can't help but think of the contrast between two of the big, whopping miracles God's people experienced in the Old Testament. The first one was when Charlton Heston . . . sorry, I mean *Moses*, raised his staff in front of the Red Sea and it parted, allowing the Israelites to evade Pharaoh's army—who were closing in behind them after the Israelites began their exodus out of Egypt. That story goes something like this:

> When word reached the king of Egypt that the Israelites had fled, Pharaoh and his officials changed their minds. "What have we done, letting all those Israelite slaves get away?" they asked. So Pharaoh harnessed his chariot and called up his troops. He took with him 600 of Egypt's best chariots, along with the rest of the chariots of Egypt, each with its commander. The LORD hardened the heart of Pharaoh, the king of Egypt, so he chased after the people of Israel, who had left with fists raised in defiance. The

Egyptians chased after them with all the forces in Pharaoh's army—all his horses and chariots, his charioteers, and his troops. The Egyptians caught up with the people of Israel as they were camped beside the shore near Pi-hahiroth, across from Baal-zephon.

As Pharaoh approached, the people of Israel looked up and panicked when they saw the Egyptians overtaking them. They cried out to the LORD, and they said to Moses, "Why did you bring us out here to die in the wilderness? Weren't there enough graves for us in Egypt? What have you done to us? Why did you make us leave Egypt? Didn't we tell you this would happen while we were still in Egypt? We said, 'Leave us alone! Let us be slaves to the Egyptians. It's better to be a slave in Egypt than a corpse in the wilderness!'"

But Moses told the people, "Don't be afraid. Just stand still and watch the LORD rescue you today. The Egyptians you see today will never be seen again. The LORD himself will fight for you. Just stay calm."

Then the LORD said to Moses, "Why are you crying out to me? Tell the people to get moving! Pick up your staff and raise your hand over the sea. Divide the water so the Israelites can walk through the middle of the sea on dry ground. And I will harden the hearts of the Egyptians, and they will charge in after the Israelites. My great glory will be displayed through

Pharaoh and his troops, his chariots, and his charioteers. When my glory is displayed through them,
all Egypt will see my glory and know that I am the
Lord!"

Then the angel of God, who had been leading the
people of Israel, moved to the rear of the camp. The
pillar of cloud also moved from the front and stood
behind them. The cloud settled between the Egyptian
and Israelite camps. As darkness fell, the cloud turned
to fire, lighting up the night. But the Egyptians and
Israelites did not approach each other all night.

Then Moses raised his hand over the sea, and
the Lord opened up a path through the water with a
strong east wind. The wind blew all that night, turning
the seabed into dry land. So the people of Israel walked
through the middle of the sea on dry ground, with
walls of water on each side! (Exodus 14:5–22 NLT)

The short version of those eighteen verses goes like this:

1. God told Pharaoh to give the Israelites a green card
   out of Egypt.
2. Pharaoh said, "Yes, sir," and let God's man Moses
   lead the Israelites out of town.
3. But then the King-Tut-ish guy changed his mind and
   gave chase. The Israelites panicked when they got to

     the ocean's edge, assuming they were toast because the Egyptian army was hot on their tail.

4. Moe said, "Quit freaking out and turn down your iPods so you can hear me give directions over this megaphone because Yahweh is going to save us!"
5. And God did.

The Israelites didn't have to bail one single bucket of water from the Red Sea to save themselves—God did all the heavy lifting. All they had to do was sit on the bank and watch while He carved out a white sandy path through the Red Sea. Then they paraded across like people who'd won the lottery without even buying a ticket!

Forty years later they reach another watery boundary called the Jordan River and this time it's a whole other story. This time God basically says, *I want you to do more than just watch*:

> Early the next morning Joshua and all the Israelites left Acacia Grove and arrived at the banks of the Jordan River, where they camped before crossing. Three days later the Israelite officers went through the camp, giving these instructions to the people: "When you see the Levitical priests carrying the Ark of the Covenant of the LORD your God, move out from your positions and follow them. Since you have

never traveled this way before, they will guide you. Stay about a half mile behind them, keeping a clear distance between you and the Ark. Make sure you don't come any closer."

Then Joshua told the people, "Purify yourselves, for tomorrow the LORD will do great wonders among you."

In the morning Joshua said to the priests, "Lift up the Ark of the Covenant and lead the people across the river." And so they started out and went ahead of the people.

The LORD told Joshua, "Today I will begin to make you a great leader in the eyes of all the Israelites. They will know that I am with you, just as I was with Moses. Give this command to the priests who carry the Ark of the Covenant: 'When you reach the banks of the Jordan River, take a few steps into the river and stop there.'"

So Joshua told the Israelites, "Come and listen to what the LORD your God says. Today you will know that the living God is among you. He will surely drive out the Canaanites, Hittites, Hivites, Perizzites, Girgashites, Amorites, and Jebusites ahead of you. Look, the Ark of the Covenant, which belongs to the Lord of the whole earth, will lead you across the Jordan River! Now choose twelve men from the tribes of Israel, one from each tribe. The priests will carry the Ark of the LORD, the Lord of all the earth. As soon as their feet touch the water, the flow of water will be cut off upstream, and the river will stand up like a wall."

So the people left their camp to cross the Jordan, and the priests who were carrying the Ark of the Covenant went ahead of them. It was the harvest season, and the Jordan was overflowing its banks. But as soon as the feet of the priests who were carrying the Ark touched the water at the river's edge, the water above that point began backing up a great distance away at a town called Adam, which is near Zarethan. And the water below that point flowed on to the Dead Sea until the riverbed was dry. Then all the people crossed over near the town of Jericho.

Meanwhile, the priests who were carrying the Ark of the LORD's Covenant stood on dry ground in the middle of the riverbed as the people passed by. They waited there until the whole nation of Israel had crossed the Jordan on dry ground. (Joshua 3:1–17 NLT)

The short version of *those* seventeen verses goes like this:

1. Moe's dead, Joshua's the man now.

....

2. God tells Josh he's about to be on the cover of *People*.
3. Josh texts the Israelites and tells them to meet him by the water's edge.
4. When the group assembles, he explains that Yahweh was planning on parting this pond too, but this time they're going to get wet.

By this chapter in their story, the Israelites have been following God's tangible presence for forty years. His Spirit hovered directly over them as a cloud during daylight hours and morphed into a pillar of fire when it got dark (Exodus 13:20–22). That's basically a blimp of supernatural guidance! Plus, He provided for every single one of their physical needs. They'd forgotten what a growling stomach sounded like (Exodus 16:1–36; Numbers 11:1–9). Jehovah even established a creative way for them to be healed from poisonous snake bites; all the Israelites had to do when bitten was look at a bronze serpent at the top of a pole in the center of camp, thereby tangibly expressing their belief in God's faithfulness, and the deadly effects of the venom would miraculously disappear (Numbers 21:8–9).

Those often obstinate and whiny Hebrews experienced Four. Long. Decades. of divine provision and protection. They were middle-aged in relationship with their Redeemer and they'd never, ever seen the righteous forsaken. So now He expects them to *participate* in the miracle instead of simply observe it. Of course being the merciful Heavenly Father that He is, God doesn't command them to climb up the high-dive ladder and do a double backflip. Nor does He make them jump into the deep end. Heck, He doesn't even ask them to take off their arm floaties. All they had to do was put their feet in the water far enough to get their ankles wet and *SHAZAAM* . . . the Jordan River split in two like a sharp knife going through a cold watermelon! It's amazing what a small amount of risk on our part God counts as being *all in*.

One of the places I've watched brave women consistently wade into scary, swirling water is a place called The Next Door. It's a faith-based, residential program in downtown Nashville for women who are recovering from drug and alcohol addictions (we've recently added two more programs in Knoxville and Chattanooga, Tennessee). I volunteer at The Next Door—teaching Bible studies, serving dinner, or just hanging out with the girls—as often as I can because it's my favorite place to observe God performing miracles. Sometimes I get my feet wet there too.

A few weeks ago, right after I got to teach a Bible study at The Next Door, one of the residents I don't know all that well walked up to me and shyly asked if I'd pray something specific for her. After I assured her that I'd be glad to, she looked directly into my eyes and with one hand in front of her mouth asked, "Will you please pray that God will get me some new teeth?" Her expression was a mixture of humility, sincerity, and cobbled-together dignity that all but slayed me. I reached for her hand and told her I was honored she would allow me to join her in praying for something so personal. And that's when the rest of her story came tumbling out.

"Maggie May" described how she'd been addicted to meth since she was a teenager. How it had robbed her of her innocence, ruined her marriage, ransacked her body, and most painfully of all, alienated her from her two children. She hasn't seen her thirteen-year-old son or her four-year-old daughter since she was incarcerated a year and a half ago.

The good news is Maggie got sober in prison and has been clean for the longest season of her adult life (she's one of many I've met who credit being behind bars as what ultimately helped them get off drugs, find Jesus, and experience true freedom). After explaining how excited she is about an upcoming family reunion, Maggie said, "Lisa, my kids never saw me smile much because I was high most of the time I was around 'em. And when I wasn't high, I was angry or crazy actin' because all I really cared about was the next hit. Now that I'm clean I want them to see me smile all the time but I'm ashamed to smile very big because I lost most of my teeth to meth. That's why I want you to pray for God to give me new teeth . . . I wanna be able to smile big at my kids."

I promised her that if she finished the program, we'd find a way to get her some teeth. Then I cried the whole way home and confessed how sorry I was that I wasn't more grateful for things like teeth and shampoo and clean sheets. I wasn't exactly sure how God was going to provide them, but at that point I was willing to give Maggie some of my own chompers. Now here's the parting-the-water part: less than a week later I shared her story at another Bible study in town and within twenty-four hours, THREE dentists had contacted me offering their services for free! Sweet Maggie is going to have a mega-kilowatt smile to share with her kids.

I've been in relationship with God now for as long as the Israelites were when they got to the Jordan and I can honestly say I've never seen the righteous forsaken either. Mind you, I've seen Christians disappointed and heart-broken. Shoot, *I've* been disappointed and heartbroken. But I've never experienced the absolute absence of God, even in my darkest hours. Which means I don't have an excuse for hugging the shoreline anymore. I'm ready to get soaked! To dive in! To legally change my name to "Agnes Jr."! Now if only I could find a flattering bathing suit.

....

4

BLASTING THROUGH BURNOUT

Quiet minds, which are established in stillness,
refuse to be perplexed or intimidated.[1]

—*Tim Hansel*

got so tickled by the side effects of my own overextension recently. But before I confess my utter
foolishness, I need to explain that it has been a *Ca.
Ray. Zee.* season. A flat-out bonkers, from-dawn-til-
dusk, racing-from–one-meeting-to-another couple of
weeks. And this particular day was the pinnacle of this
warp-speed chunk of calendar because I was scheduled

to make a presentation of the very book you have in your hot little hands to a roomful of movers and shakers in the publishing world.

Well, of course I didn't schedule quite enough of a buffer between a morning business rendezvous and the luncheon/presentation session. So I came rushing into the big-wig shindig a few minutes late and several cups of coffee short of serene. My hair had been blown into a disheveled, Medusa-like mess in the windy parking lot, and I was noticeably out of breath from the stairs. Needless to say, my tardy appearance was less than elegant.

Thankfully, I immediately recognized two safe friends, Matt and Andy, when I entered the room and made a beeline for them, assuming I'd have a few minutes to settle down in their brotherly midst. But when I approached them, I realized there was a third guy engaged in their circle of conversation, a grinning bald man I didn't recognize. After Matt and Andy greeted me, this kind stranger grabbed me in an exuberant hug and kissed me on both cheeks. Then he continued sharing a personal story and looked at me warmly a few times, as if I was already privy to his anecdote. As if we were old friends.

As an older single chick, I'm usually delighted by unexpected smooches from friendly fellows. However, this man's greeting and persona were so inclusive that I couldn't help fretting, *"Oh crud, this is obviously someone I've met before at Thomas Nelson or HarperCollins and I can't for the life of me remember who he is or where we first met!"* Although I smiled and nodded as if I was comfy as a bug in a rug while Mr. Cheerful kept chatting, worried thoughts were flashing through my frazzled mind: *Is he one of those savvy marketing guys from New York? Maybe he's the one who e-mailed me about video rights? Have I been to a party at his house? Yikes, is he someone I was supposed to follow up with after one of those meetings with Zondervan in Michigan? Yikers, I might be so fired if he figures out I don't have a clue who he is.*

Then, just before my brain overheated from trying to recall his identity, a pensive thought wafted through my brain: *Boy, he sure does look like that guy from* The Love Boat. At which point, I took a mental field trip from the conversation he, Matt, and Andy were having and began reminiscing about my favorite episodes. About Gopher, the often-hapless second-in-command and Julie, the cruise ship hostess with the most-est. Thirty seconds later, when *The Love Boat* theme song began reverberating in my head, I had a brow-raising epiphany—this smiling, effusive stranger *was* Captain Steubing! It turns out the oh-so-gracious actor, Gavin MacLeod, was pitching his new book project right after mine.

Now, while being enveloped by a sitcom star I don't recognize isn't a common occurrence for me, being frazzled is. I often find myself mentally stretched, physically taxed, and emotionally chaffed. Frankly, I think most women between the ages of eighteen and eighty do. And since many of the factors contributing to our oft-frazzled condition aren't within the purview of our preference—in other words, we can't truly control death, traffic, viruses, or people—let's consider a practical and effective method to survive and even thrive in the lovely madness of our lives.

Breathe

The first step to walking well through busy days and even *Ca. Ray. Zee.* seasons is to *breathe*. I know that sounds like a no-brainer. I mean, we have to ingest copious amounts of a carbon-and-oxygen mixture in order to live regardless of what's on the calendar, right? Well, yeah, but I've learned that the *way* we breathe, especially during periods of stress, is very important. Simply being intentional about the way I inhale and exhale has had a profound effect on how smoothly I navigate busyness. As a matter of fact, had I taken half a minute to actually live what I'm about to preach, I probably would've thoroughly enjoyed that conversational voyage with the captain of the Love Boat. And how much more significant is it for us to enjoy our journey with the Captain of the Whole World?

Here's the deal. The next time you find yourself both overextended and overwhelmed, try the following: take five deep breaths and during each breathing sequence concentrate on *inhaling God's peace* and *exhaling anxiety*. If you're new to what I like to call "divine deep breathing," it might help you to repeat the below instructions in your head while responding to them with your body. Just focus on taking as big a breath as you can, holding it for five seconds, then exhaling until you've expired most of the air in your lungs.

Inhale God's peace (hold that breath for five seconds, form your lips into a relaxed puffer fish pose, blow slowly). Exhale anxiety.

Inhale God's peace. Exhale anxiety.

Inhale God's peace. Exhale anxiety.

Inhale God's peace. Exhale anxiety.

Inhale God's peace. Exhale anxiety.

A few months ago, I spent three days shooting my first video-based Bible study with LifeWay. Of course, I planned to lose ten pounds before the recording, but I didn't. So I had the misfortune of being crammed into a pair of Spanx, which were noticeably worn, so I kept worrying, *If this fancy girdle rips, somebody's bound to lose an eye*. Plus, I planned on taking a week off prior to filming in order to be really relaxed and prepared when the cameras started rolling. But alas, I'd flown in from a teaching engagement the night before. To say that *Malachi*[2] shoot was a *little* stressful is like saying a grizzly is a *little* hungry when it wakes up from hibernating all winter.

After the shooting finally wrapped, I drove home with my sunroof open so I could hold my hands up at red lights and passionately praise God, because it was only by His grace that we didn't have any major train wrecks while filming. Although I created a huge workload for the poor editors (several of whom have expressed appreciation for the way I provide them with job security), I didn't use any expletives or accidentally shatter an expensive camera on set.

By the time I got home I was whistling. I basically skipped to the back door, and then my heart skipped a beat when I noticed a gorgeous flower arrangement the delivery guy had left on the porch. I picked it up—inhaling the sweet scent of fresh blooms—and opened the accompanying note: "Congratulations, now *breathe!* Love, Beth and Priscilla." Beth Moore and Priscilla Shirer are two of the godliest women I know, and since they both emphasize the importance of breathing during busy seasons, you can bet your bottom dollar it's a theologically sound strategy!

Listen

The Old Testament book of Isaiah gives us the second clue regarding how to sail through *Ca.Ray.Zee.* seasons without overturning:

> And your ears shall hear a word behind you, saying, "This is the way, walk in it," when you turn to the right or when you turn to the left. (Isaiah 30:21)

In other words, God gives us specific directions—even when life is loud and chaotic. All we have to do is *listen*.

I hate to admit it, but the most recent place I heard divine GPS (I've intentionally rechristened that term to mean "God's Positioning System" because the lady who lives in my dashboard has an annoying voice unlike the pleasant tone of the Holy Spirit in my head) was in the drive-thru line at Taco Bell. Or as I prefer to call it, Taco *Smell*. If you're ever desperate enough to eat one of their burritos, the odor will seep into your hands and linger, thereby shaming you about your digression into teenage-boy-fast-foodom for days!

Well, anyway, I was in a hurry as usual and the joint that blessed the world with the bazillion-calorie-Doritos-inspired taco was the only place I had time to grab a bite before racing into another meeting. So I wheeled into their drive-thru with the thought: *I think there's some little bean thingy on their menu that's only like ten points at Weight Watchers.* And while I was pondering the I-bet-this-makes-real-Mexicans-wince list on the menu in front of me, a very sweet voice piped out of the metal talk box: "Welcome to Taco Bell, may I take your order, please?" I was surprised by the genuine kindness in the disembodied voice so I said, "You sure can! I want one of those little plain bean burritos and a Diet Pepsi, please." Then I pulled around the corner to meet the person the voice lived in.

The first thing I noticed was that she had a wide smile, which in my experience is an atypical expression for a teenager working the drive-thru window. I'm more used to sullen and clipped with a side order of rolled eyes. In that exact moment, I sensed God poking me and whispering, *She could use a little encouragement today, Lisa.* So, I said, "You have a great voice and a wonderful smile, what's your name?" To which, she grinned wider and said, "My name is Leondria." I asked, "Lee-Own-Dree-Ah?" She replied firmly, "No, Lee-Awn-Dree-Uh." And I said, "Oh . . . your mama sure was creative!" Which I hoped made up for my abysmal ability to pronounce urban names. Then I said, "Lee-Awn-Dree-Uh, you remind me of a verse in the Bible that says, 'Those who look to him are radiant; their faces are never covered with shame' (Psalm 34:5 NIV)."

Of course, we'd only known each other for thirty

seconds, so I wasn't sure how well the affirmation would go over. But then in a tumble of words Leondria told me it was her eighteenth birthday and she'd been bummed all afternoon because she really wanted to be hanging out with her friends instead of being stuck in a Taco Bell drive-thru. She explained that she'd just been thinking, *Lawd, I need some kind of reminder that you see me today because this ain't exactly how I wanted to spend my birthday,* before I appeared. Her eyes lit up as she exclaimed, "Then he sent me YOU to remind me of how special I am!" And for a minute there I thought she was going to try and squeeze through that itty-bitty window to hug me.

The next time you're feeling flummoxed by the length of your to-do list, just *breathe*, then lean in and *listen* for God's directions. He might tell you to be still . . . or He might just guide you to do some small something for someone else before tackling your own seemingly gigantic stuff!

Ask

The third step of the staying-calm-even-when-life-is-hectic waltz is to *ask*. Once we've taken five divine deep breaths and listened to the Holy Spirit, we need to ask God for clarity regarding our current circumstances. Because often when we're feeling frazzled, the stress we're experiencing is less about what's taking place in that moment and more about baggage we're still lugging from the past. Trust me on this, I've paid one hundred dollars an hour for years in order to speak from experience on this one.

For example, when I was a little girl I overheard a lot of loud fighting between grown-ups. On several sad occasions, I was in the room when the yelling escalated into hitting. Once, the hitting got so bad that I jumped in between my mama and the man who was slamming her head into the floor. I was four years old when I shielded my mom and cried, "Please don't hit her anymore" to the angry man. And while those violent episodes are a long time gone, I can still remember them as if they happened yesterday. It's as if they made handprints in the wet cement of my childish heart, and those indentations still collect water when it rains in my adult life. Consequently, I'm still wary when I'm around someone who acts mad. Even safe people who are expressing healthy anger or just enthused irritability.

This kind of thing happened recently while I was with one of my mom friends. We'd been merrily cruising along in her van when her boys began to roughhouse in the backseat. She calmly requested, "Please quit punching your brother." But she might as well have been speaking Greek because her seven- and nine-year-old completely ignored her. She shot me an apologetic look when we pulled up to the next red light, then wheeled around and jabbed a warning finger toward her rambunctious children—who were of course feigning innocence now. She bellowed firmly, "If y'all don't behave and stop pummeling each other, you're both going to have a very long time-out when we get home!" After her ominous and obviously legitimate warning, calm descended on our convoy like a soft blanket of snow . . . yet it still made me a tad nervous.

Typically, the louder a voice gets, the bigger the knot in my gut grows. So I have to turn my heart and mind toward our Heavenly Father and ask, "Is this pit in my stomach about *today* or is it about what *already happened* in the past or about what I'm afraid *might happen* in the future?" Taking a moment to ask God for clarity usually leads to an unruffled awareness about what's really going on. It's taken me decades to get this, but I'm finally learning that extremely intense emotions—like panic or fury—are often rooted in the past or flung toward the unknowable future. Whereas more reasonable responses—like when a mother dispenses discipline without totally losing her cool, or when a couple argues without abusing or devaluing one another—tend to be based in current reality. If you live long enough, disappointment is inevitable. Drama, on the other hand, isn't.

. . . .

And, let's not forget, most of what we're afraid *might happen* never actually does. My friend Angie will tell how she can invest gobs of energy worrying about whether or not our plane will crash when we're traveling to and from Women of Faith events, yet the probability of being killed in an airplane crash is one in 4.7 million.[3] And I've invested countless hours worrying about how chunky I look, yet I've never been forced to step on a scale or pirouette in my undies before going to the movies or hanging out with friends (obviously I don't count Weight Watchers or Jenny Craig as pleasant social outings because, in my opinion, they're on the same dubious list as root canals and colonoscopies).

Now, if anyone really earned the "right" to go to counseling, it was Jesus' human family from Nazareth. And I think his half brother James did, because he preaches the importance of emotional awareness—of paying close attention to how *God's promises* apply to our *personal stories*:

> Those who hear God's teaching and do nothing are like people who look at themselves in a mirror. They see their faces and then go away and quickly forget what they looked like. But the truly happy people are those who carefully study God's perfect law that makes people free, and they continue to study it.

They do not forget what they heard, but they obey what God's teaching says. Those who do this will be made happy. (James 1:23–25 NCV)

We aren't supposed to completely ignore the handprints that were made in our particular cement. Remembering the yesterdays God rescued us from will ensure they don't mar our todays. As far as tomorrow goes, there's no need to worry about it. Matt says it best: "Therefore do not worry about tomorrow, for tomorrow will worry about itself. Each day has enough trouble of its own" (Matthew 6:34 NIV). But we can rest assured that our Shepherd has every single second mapped out. And when it comes to our present circumstances, let's *ask* God for clarity, help, and wisdom so as to keep both feet firmly planted in the *now* of our lives.

Smile

The fourth action to take when we find ourselves approaching the curve of burnout is the easiest: *smile.* I believe it's close to miraculous what simply curling the edge of our lips upward can do for our hearts. Frankly, I'm convinced there's a correlation, because when my mouth forms into a real smile it doesn't simply cause a twinkle in my eyes, it permeates my whole body. Even the worry lines in my soul begin to plump up and disappear when treated with a genuine grin.

Smiling doesn't cost a cent. There's no prescription for it, and it's not nearly as taxing as Zumba. Furthermore, while the old adage that it takes fewer muscles to smile than it does to frown isn't based on science or anatomical fact (it actually takes a few more muscles to smile), smiling often takes less effort because we tend to use those facial muscles more frequently. And, interestingly, smart guys have proven that when a control group was instructed to make an expression of anger, fear, sadness, or disgust, they experienced accompanying negative physical reactions like sweating and an increased heart rate, even though they *knew* they were pretending! Conversely, when a control group was told to smile, they were gauged as feeling happier than the grumpy actors, even though they were only fake-smiling![14]

The bottom line is that if we want to stop perspiring like a sumo wrestler in a sauna and decrease our I'm-close-to-having-a-heart-attack symptoms when we're under duress, then we need to start smiling! I bought a cute wooden plaque the other day to put in my little girl's room that reads, "You make me smile all over my face." I think it would do all of us good to practice that pose.

....

Take the Next Step

The final move—the *grand jete*, if you will—of our resisting-the-urge-to-become-overwhelmed-when-we're-overextended routine is to simply *take the next step*. I'm guilty of trying to run before I walk and therefore often get way ahead of myself. I also tend to bust down doors that aren't actually locked when I'm feeling harried. If only I'd taken the time to *breathe, listen, ask,* and *smile* I probably would've realized I could've just turned the knob and stepped casually into the next room!

I've also experienced the opposite reaction of being so overcome by the steady onslaught of life that instead of forging blindly ahead, I become paralyzed. Several years ago I found myself so emotionally debilitated that I was having a hard time getting out of bed in the morning. I hadn't struggled with acute depression before, but after soldiering on through the deaths of several loved ones and a cancer scare of my own, my get-up-and-go was totally gone. All I wanted to do was wave a white flag at life, crawl under the covers, and only come out of my cave long enough to order a pizza and maybe watch a few episodes of *Man Vs Wild*.

If someone had given me a perky acrostic or suggested that I listen to a sermon titled, "Thirty Things Victorious Christians Should Do to Kick Depression to the Curb,"

I think I would've kicked them in the shins. Fortunately, the counselor I've gone to for years doesn't prescribe the dangerous meds of *minimalizing grief* or *multiplying guilt*. Instead, she listened to every single word I said about why I was feeling so completely defeated and disabled. And she was appropriately silent and empathetic when I sobbed, handing me Kleenex instead of pithy, inspirational quotes.

After spilling my guts and drenching Lynn's carpet with tears I asked her for advice, and she said, "Just do the next right thing." She encouraged me not to try to tackle the troubles of an entire day, much less a week or a month, but simply to take one step forward. Some days that meant I woke up to the harsh buzz of the alarm clock, followed by knee-buckling emotional agony when I became coherent enough to remember my circumstances, and then spoke the name "Jesus" out loud three or four times in the dark. Somehow just saying the name of our Savior gave me enough courage to pull the covers back and stumble to the bathroom to brush my teeth. After rinsing the toothpaste out of my mouth, I'd stand up and recite the passage posted on the chalkboard beside the sink:

> He says, "Don't be afraid, because I have saved you. I have called you by name, and you are mine. When you pass through the waters, I will be with you. When you cross rivers, you will not drown. When you walk

through fire, you will not be burned, nor will the flames hurt you. This is because I, the LORD, am your God, the Holy One of Israel, your Savior. (Isaiah 43:1b–3a NCV)

Then I'd take a shower and recite a laminated prayer I have posted in there. After I toweled off, I'd turn on some worship music, and so on. God took me by the hand and led me through that sorrowful valley of life one step at a time. And I think that's the part where so many of us get tripped up. When life is tough or taxing, it doesn't mean we should try to bust through it like a linebacker trying to flatten a three-hundred-pound defensive tackle. Nor does it mean we can bury our head under the covers and the hard or hectic parts will disappear. Instead, we have to put our hand into the outstretched, nail-scarred palm of our Redeemer and allow Him to lead us. Sometimes that means simply doing the *Next. Right. Thing.* Just put one foot in front of the other and move . . . a little forward momentum is often all it takes to rock out of an overwhelmed rut.

I don't know if you've noticed, but the acrostic for thriving in tense times spells the word *blast*. And while I usually have the same aversion to acrostics that I have for Christmas theme sweaters, I've grown fond of this one. Because **B** (for *breathing*), **L** (for *listening*), **A** (for *asking*), **S** (for *smiling*), and **T** (for *taking the next step*) helps me remember that a saturated calendar doesn't have to be stressful. We really can have a blast during busy seasons and enjoy every minute God allows us to take up space on this planet.

Before you turn the page, I'd like to make one last suggestion: look at the calendar on your iPhone, Blackberry, desk, or refrigerator and locate the busiest, most potentially stressful day that's looming in the near future. Now with that *Ca. Ray. Zee.* day in mind, practice having a *b.l.a.s.t!*

5

CAN A BROKEN HEART
STILL BREATHE?

The most privileged, comfortable person . . . from the best
family, has already suffered the torments of the damned.
I don't think any of us get off this planet without suffering
enormously. And one of the chief ways we suffer is by
loving people who are incredibly limited by the fact that
they're human beings, and they're going to disappoint
us and break our hearts . . . We are all heartbroken.[1]

—*Mary Karr*

By mid February 2012, I was finally allowing myself
to feel a little hopeful about bringing Anna Price
home to Tennessee. Of course, I knew the adoption wasn't a done deal. In fact, there was usually some

new Marie drama that involved impending doom with each new day. So I told my friends not to throw any baby showers, and I didn't paint a bedroom pink or buy a crib. Yet it was as if someone kept adding air to the balloon of expectant joy in my chest, because it got bigger and bigger as the clock ticked toward what appeared to be Anna P's imminent birth.

February 13, 2012

Dear Ones,

Yesterday was my first weekend day off in quite awhile so I went for a long hike in a beautiful wilderness area with my dog, Cookie. It was cold and peaceful and I let her romp ahead and lead us wherever she wanted. So of course we ended up following a wild animal—it was either a rabbit or a turkey, but I only saw a flash of wildlife fanny so I can't be sure which—down a wooded ridge to a creek. Then we traipsed along a muddy trail for a while until we wound up in a field dotted with daffodils.

At which point, Cookie sat down on her haunches and looked up at me with an expression dog owners would recognize as pure joy.

....

I plopped down next to her and felt my heart curve into a grin too, because those brave little flowers looked like they were sticking their yellow tongues out at the drab gray of winter!

I'm so grateful for the blooms of hope that keep popping up in this adoption story. Like the fact that Anna Price's heart and lungs are strong in spite of Marie's crack use. Like the fact that precious little punkin' has fought to stay in the womb now for thirty-three and a half weeks. Like the fact that her equally precious biological mom visited a drug rehab facility with Andrea after her doctor's appointment last Thursday. Marie isn't willing to check herself in yet, but at least she's acknowledging her addiction.

In three to four weeks, the temperature will be warmer, the sun will set later, tulips will be blooming here in Tennessee, and a baby girl will be born in Florida. A baby girl I can totally picture toddling along behind Cookie! In the meantime, we can hope and pray and enjoy the audacity of daffodils.

Warmest Regards,
Lisa

Verses for the Week: "We also have joy with our troubles, because we know that these troubles produce patience. And patience produces character, and character produces hope. And this hope will never disappoint us, because God has poured out his love to fill our hearts." (Romans 5:3–5a NCV)

P.S. We found out last week that my mom, Patti Angel, has a large tumor in her bladder. I would appreciate it if you would pray for her as well when you pray for Marie and Anna Price (we don't know if the tumor is cancerous or benign yet). Again, "thank you" falls far short of expressing my gratitude that you continue to carry us to the throne of God's grace and mercy.

February 20, 2012

Dear Fellow Sojourners,

My social worker told me recently that studies have shown the estrogen levels of older chicks like me can increase to those of a pregnant woman during the adoption process. I'm hoping this explains my eight-pound weight gain since

Christmas. And my heaving sobs while watching *The Voice* last week. If this baby doesn't come pretty soon, I'm going to be schlepping around in elastic-waist pants with a permanent box of Kleenex in my hand!

Yet thanks to God's infinite grace—illuminated by your prayers—Anna Price is still yawning, stretching, rolling, and kicking in Marie's womb. In light of the drug-induced chaos surrounding her, it's a miracle that scrappy little punkin' has made it to thirty-four and a half weeks in utero! That both she and her precious biological mama are still okay. So regardless of how the next chapter plays out, there is much to praise our Redeemer for in this story.

But my goodness, what a wild ride it has been!

Last week it looked as if I was being completely written out of the story. I'm not at liberty to share details, but suffice it to say because of extenuating circumstances and other people in Marie's life, I had to lay down my desire to adopt Anna Price and essentially step back in the palms-up posture of surrender. I had to stand behind the God Malachi refers to as "the Lord of Heaven's Armies" (1:8 NLT) and trust Him to fight a battle that was way too big for the dinky, plastic sword

I wield. And fight God did! He conquered seemingly insurmountable odds and enabled me to stay in Marie and Anna Price's story.

The last four months have proven I'm not exactly gifted when it comes to walking behind the Creator and Commander of the Universe. In fact, I have a tendency to charge ahead of Him in most situations and then wonder why my heart, mind, and spirit get all bruised and bloody. I'm what you could call trust-challenged! But I'm learning. Slowly but surely, our tender Savior is teaching me to LAY. IT. ALL. DOWN. To live every day—regardless of whether things are playing out the way I want them to—like I really believe that God's ways are perfect. That He will meet all our needs according to His glorious riches in Christ Jesus. That His boundaries fall in pleasant places. That He will ultimately work everything out for our good and His glory.

In the meantime, I can't tell you how much I appreciate your willingness to pray for Marie to find hope and healing in Jesus and get free from her addiction to crack. For soon-to-be-born Anna Price to be healthy and whole. And for me to trust God, quit boohooing, and lay off the carbs. :)

....

Gratefully,
Lisa

Verse for the Week: "The ways of God are without fault; the LORD's words are pure. He is a shield to those who trust him." (2 Samuel 22:31 NCV)

P.S. Thank you for praying for my mom, Patti, as well. We found out on Thursday that her tumor is much bigger than the doctor originally thought and involves both her bladder and colon. However, we're very grateful it seems to be contained. And we believe God will enable the surgeon to remove the entire mass. Until then, she and I are passing notes back and forth in our remedial "walk behind God" class!

February 27, 2012

Dear Anna Price Home Team,

Yesterday I got to watch twelve women place their broken hearts in God's healing hands for the first time. I was overwhelmed by the tangible grace He lavished on us at this particular event. Then, when I was walking on air toward my car in

....

the church parking lot, I got a text explaining that two police officers and a sheriff's deputy had visited Marie's residence because of suspected drug activity. While I was dancing for joy in a sanctuary in Huntsville, Alabama, she was admitting to smoking crack again and undergoing prenatal stress tests at a Central Florida hospital to make sure Anna Price was still alive in her belly.

Dancing and weeping. Hope and despair. Joy and sorrow. It's interesting how closely the highs and lows of life coexist. Philosophizing aside, the great news is that Anna Price is not only still alive—she seems to be thriving! She's thirty-five and a half weeks and continues to fight for life in what doctors call an "inhospitable" environment. I won't be surprised if she's born holding a tiny sword and shield because she is a warrior! If I get to be her mama, I think I'm going to nickname her "The Anniator" and dress her in superhero onesies to celebrate her fighting spirit. She is a very brave, very determined little girl.

But I'm sure that described Marie as a baby as well. She had to be brave because her biological parents were homeless heroin addicts who exploited her for drug money. When she was rescued by the Department of Children's Services as a toddler, she had several sexually transmitted diseases. Then she was in foster care for five years. Surely she had to fight to survive there too. But now she's twenty-three and has an arrest record, a hardcore cocaine habit, a crooked jaw (from being punched in the face by a john), and several regular "customers"—men who pay for sex with her even though she's mentally impaired and eight months pregnant (I can't help but pray for God to lock men like that up in tiny, windowless rooms with a herd of goats afflicted with irritable bowel syndrome). Frankly, I think Marie is probably too tired to fight anymore.

So please help us—Andrea, the Director of the Crisis Pregnancy Center, her team, and me—slug away on her behalf. Please continue to charge God's throne of mercy with the request for Him to pull her out of the pit of abuse and addiction she's stuck in. I am deeply concerned about this bound, formerly brave little girl's future. When I first walked into her story in October, my hope was to see two lives redeemed. For both Anna Price and Marie to make it. For both of them to have joyful, healthy, and abundant lives. That's still my hope.

By the amazing grace of the God Who Is,

......

high-risk obstetric specialists have predicted that Anna Price is going to make it. That it's likely she'll be born relatively healthy and remarkably whole in two to four weeks. Forty-eight hours after birth is when I'll know whether or not I get to bring her home to Tennessee. I can hardly believe that day is right around the corner and I'll definitely keep you posted.

Warmest Regards,
Lisa

Verse for the Week: "Love is never tired of waiting." (1 Corinthians 13:4 BBE)

March 5, 2012

Dear Friends and Extended Family,

I want to begin this last Marie Monday update by thanking you for praying and writing letters and fasting for a young woman you've never met and her soon-to-be-born baby girl, who I was going to name Anna Price. Even for a verbose woman like me, words fail to express the depth of gratitude I have for each of you. I believe your prayers have

....

helped keep Anna Price alive for the last tumultuous few months and I know your letters have
helped Marie move closer toward the love of God.

The reason this will be my last update is because
Marie's adoptive parents (who were initially very
supportive of me being the adoptive mom) have
decided they want to have legal guardianship of
the baby after all. So they drove to Florida a few
days ago and took Marie back to Colorado with
them, in effect nullifying the adoption plans.

Just as I don't have words to express how
grateful I am for your support, neither do I have
adequate words to express my disappointment. It
feels like a boulder has rolled over my heart. But in
light of the baby's survival (she's now at thirty-six
and a half weeks, which is more time in utero than
we even prayed for, therefore she should be born
healthy and strong sometime this month in spite
of her mama's crack addiction) and Marie's growing understanding of God's grace, the past four
months have been worth it. I know God is sovereign and good and His ways are perfect even
though this story hasn't turned out at all the way
I hoped it would. And as C. S. Lewis so beautifully
explained, I truly believe it's better to have a broken heart than one that's unbreakable:

Love anything, and your heart will certainly be wrung and positively broken. If you want to make sure of keeping it intact, you must give your heart to no one, not even to an animal. Wrap it carefully round with hobbies and little luxuries; avoid all entanglements; lock it up safe in the casket or coffin of your selfishness. But in that casket—safe, dark, motionless, airless—it will change. It will not be broken; it will become unbreakable, impenetrable, irredeemable. The alternative to tragedy, or at least to the risk of tragedy, is damnation.[2]

When I find out the baby is here, safe and sound, I'll let you know.

Gratefully,

Lisa

Verse for the Week: "The LORD is close to the brokenhearted, and he saves those whose spirits have been crushed." (Psalm 34:18 EXB)

I don't think I'll ever forget the day my dream of being Anna Price's mom died. I was sitting on the couch with my laptop, returning e-mails, when my cell phone rang, and I noticed the caller was my adoption agency in Florida. A lump immediately welled up in my throat when I answered it because I was afraid it was going to be bad news. They'd only called a few times before and it was never good news. So I stood up and began pacing.

Surprisingly, the social worker's voice was light and positive and she told me she was just calling to let me know that *everything was in place.* She said the baby was due in about two weeks and I needed to go ahead and arrange to be in Florida for the second half of March because barring an unforeseen curveball, I was going to be a mom!

She went on to explain that Marie had signed all the necessary paperwork and continued to be steadfast in her desire for me to be Anna Price's adoptive mom. Then she described how the State of Florida was officially giving the agency (in effect, me) temporary guardianship rather than placing the baby in temporary foster care when she was born. This is because state law prohibits biological moms with illegal drugs in their system to take their newborns home from the hospital, and Marie's blood work proved her to be an ongoing drug user. Which meant I'd be able to take Anna Price home from the hospital. I'd get to change her first diaper. I'd get to feed her the first bottle. I'd get to watch her sleep in the precious white bassinet with a canopy that my

Aunt Darlene had already set up in their guestroom for us. I just couldn't leave the state until the final adoption paperwork was complete forty-eight hours after her birth. I thought, *No big deal. All I want to do is hold her . . . it doesn't matter where.*

After congratulating me and asking me to e-mail my itinerary, she said goodbye. I plopped back down on the couch with a sigh. And then buckets of tears began streaming down my face. Before I knew it, I was crying so hard I had to put my head in my hands. Soon the sobs became interspersed with laughter. My shoulders shook and my nose ran and my heart did cartwheels around the living room chanting, *Anna Price is coming home! Anna Price is coming home! Anna Price is coming home!* Relief took on a whole new meaning for me because I'd never experienced it wearing a cheerleading uniform and twirling a baton before.

I was so joyfully discombobulated that I started praising the Lord really loud and scared my poor dogs! Then I called my family and closest friends and babbled the great news between more happy-crying spells.

That afternoon I noticed my adoption agency flashing on my cell phone again so I said, "Hello," cheerfully, with no lump. I assumed she'd just forgotten to tell me about a form she needed me to sign and scan back to her or something. But it was immediately apparent by the tone of her voice that something was wrong. *Very wrong.*

. . . .

I'm not at liberty to go into detail, but due to circumstances beyond our control, the bottom fell out of my dream. I was not going to get to bring Anna Price home to Tennessee. Marie was not going to rehab. And I wasn't going to be a mama anytime soon. Friends of mine who've experienced both late-term miscarriages and failed adoptions tell me the grief is similar. Each of those losses leaves the same-shaped hole in your heart. All I know is that I felt like I'd been punched in the stomach. Hard. It felt like the wind had been knocked out of my life.

While I was still reeling, the phone rang again. This time it was my mom calling on the way home from her surgeon's office. He had just informed her the tumor in her abdomen was not only malignant, it was Stage Four and the cancer had metastasized to more major organs than he originally thought. He wanted to schedule surgery immediately and his prognosis regarding her future health was sobering.

Early in the evening, Dad called. By that point I was so wrung out, so tired of crying, that I didn't have the energy to tell him what had taken place that day. I thought, *I'll tell him about Anna Price and mom tomorrow, but right now I'm just going to ask him a few questions and keep the conversation short.* So I casually asked, "How ya doin, Dad?" He paused for a second or two and then said, "I'm not doing very well, honey, because I went to the doctor this afternoon."

I queried back, "What'd he say, Dad?" And he told me the doctor read the results of his latest scan which revealed the cancer they'd operated on twice before had spread to his lungs and liver and there was nothing more they could do surgically. They informed him that he had about two months to live unless he chose to go through another round of radically aggressive chemotherapy. Even then the doctor said he'd probably only gain another few months.

I prayed for Dad over the phone, told him I loved him very much, promised I'd call him the next day after I talked to his doctor myself, and then hung up the phone. I sat on the bed for several minutes in shock, completely stunned by the devastation of the day. I wasn't sure what to do or where to turn. My mind felt sluggish and full, as if it couldn't digest another morsel of sadness.

Eventually I leaned over and robotically set the alarm for four o'clock the next morning because it vaguely occurred to me that I had an early flight. Then I remembered why. I was scheduled to speak to a group of ministry leaders in Kansas on the subject of "Keep on Keeping On." It was supposed to be a message about how we can persevere in our calling as Christ's ambassadors because of the unwavering goodness of God. *Oh, good night*, I thought. *What in the world am I going to say tomorrow when all I want to do is pull the covers over my head and not come out for a long, long time?*

....

All I had the strength to do was lie down and breathe, and even then it felt as if there were an elephant on my chest. *Breathe in God's peace . . . exhale anxiety. Breathe in God's peace . . . exhale anxiety. Breathe in God's peace . . . exhale anxiety. Breathe in God's peace . . . exhale anxiety.* After what felt like a week of grieving in the dark, the alarm began to buzz. I got up and walked to the bathroom and prayed. One step followed another, after another, after another, until fifteen hours later I was standing on a stage in downtown Kansas City overlooking a sea of expectant faces.

After taking another deep breath to steady myself, I began talking about the sovereign mercy of God. How His providence will never take us to a place where His grace is not sufficient. About how our Creator Redeemer is perfectly loving and faithful even when our lives are one hot mess . . . even when our dreams have been shattered into a million shards. And you know what? I meant every single word I said that night. I meant them because I've lived them. It may just have been the truest testimony I've ever shared.

It's one thing to talk about the joy of being *all in* for Jesus when you're in a double-espresso, good-hair, everything's-working-out-like-I-wanted-it-to kind of season. It's easy to gallop willy-nilly toward the throne of God and throw candy-coated proverbs to people sitting on the curb watching your blessed and highly favored parade pass by. Things like: *You just put that worry rock back in your pocket because everything's going to work out for the best!* (Someone actually said that to me recently. Fortunately, it was over the phone so I was unable to smack her.) But it's not nearly as easy to gallop toward God and overextend yourself toward others when life karate chops your dreams in half. Or when you barely have enough strength to put gauze on your own hemorrhaging heart.

However, I'm learning that, much like the inverted spiritual truism in chapter 1—"part of the blessing is in the stretch itself"—so also does great *joy* grow in the soil of *sorrow*. In fact, I'm not sure one can exist without the other in this life because the human heart is wired so as to need the contrast. If we didn't have dark nights, we couldn't experience the peachy glow of sunrise. If we didn't ache, we couldn't experience relief. If we didn't suffer brokenness, we couldn't experience restoration.

This symbiotic relationship between joy and sorrow means overextension will sometimes be incredibly painful for us. Stretching toward God and others when our own souls feel black-and-blue hurts. But as Mr. Lewis so wisely said, a heart that is protected from the possibility of breakage "will become unbreakable, impenetrable, irre-deemable." And that really would be the bigger tragedy.

I'd much rather risk the disappointment of love lost than never experience love at all. So, for now, I'm choosing to limp forward and hum Habakkuk's song:

Though the fig tree should not blossom, nor fruit be on the vines, the produce of the olive fail and the fields yield no food, the flock be cut off from the fold and there be no herd in the stalls, yet I will rejoice in the LORD; I will take joy in the God of my salvation. GOD, the Lord, is my strength; he makes my feet like the deer's; he makes me tread on my high places. (Habakkuk 3:17–19)

6

FATTENING UP OUR LOVE CAPACITY

When we were children, we used to think that
when we were grown-up we would no longer
be vulnerable. But to grow up is to accept
vulnerability. To be alive is to be vulnerable.[1]

—*Madeleine L'Engle*

This past New Year's Eve I wrote down four goals. I
don't like to use the word *resolution* on December
31st because I think it has more of a grit-your-
teeth-and-get-it-done implication than the hopeful spirit

I want to carry into a New Year. *Resolution* sounds too much like a diet strategy to me. Anyway these were my four goals:

- Love bigger
- Fear smaller
- Run headlong into the arms of Jesus every single day
- Become my little girl's mama

All three are important aspirations. The last one makes me teary because the finalization of my adoption is close but still uncertain, and meanwhile, my little girl's still sleeping in a shack in Haiti. But the second one, "fear smaller," is actually the one that's stuck to the edge of my soul like a burr. This is interesting, considering that until a few years ago I didn't even know that I *was* fearful. It wasn't until I was in my forties I became aware of this. Before, I'd assumed I was simply an outgoing, happy-go-lucky type of girl. At least that's how mom always described me.

In fact, she'll tell you that I basically came out of the womb with a hand out and a "Hello, My Name Is" sticker plastered on my wee chest. One of her favorite stories involves how as a baby I would hold up my arms and grin at anyone who passed by my crib or stroller, basically begging to be picked up and played with. She said it used to worry her that a stranger could easily nab me if she weren't paying attention. Mind you, we weren't famous or wealthy, so I wouldn't have been a good kidnapping candidate, but mom grew up in the aftermath of the Lindbergh tragedy, so she had an active imagination about such things.

Soon enough I graduated from being an affable infant to a smiley, sociable kid. So sociable, in fact, that it never occurred to me *not* to peddle my homemade Christmas ornaments to the Israels, a lovely Jewish family who lived a few houses down the street from us. And when Mrs. Israel politely explained they didn't celebrate Christmas, I asked her if I could come inside and talk with her about their oversight because I didn't want them to miss out on the most wonderful time of year!

Then, when I was a senior in high school, I was so friendly that I accidently flashed a football stadium filled with folks. I was riding on the back of a convertible Corvette during the halftime homecoming festivities because I was on the "white" homecoming court. (Can you believe our public high school actually had a segregated homecoming court in 1981? Thankfully that idiotic "tradition" ended a few years later.) Now, giving an exuberant extrovert the opportunity to be front and center in a parade of any sort is just asking for trouble. You might as well give a Southerner free tickets to a fried chicken, sweet tea, and banana pudding buffet. I was so excited about waving to the crowd on that fateful October evening I forgot to hold on. So when the guy driving our escort car stepped on the accelerator, I fell backward, and the wind caught the hem of my dress and blew it over my head.

Of course, in that moment I was more concerned about getting the material out of my eyes so I could see and scramble back into the car instead of becoming one with the gravelly track. It wasn't until ten or fifteen seconds later, when I was breathing heavily with relief in the safety of the burgundy leather backseat, that I realized the stands were roaring with laughter over my unintentional exhibitionism!

Needless to say, people have always been preeminent in my life. Tall, short, thin, round, pale, brown, sophisticated city dwellers, or four-wheel-driving rednecks—I like most all of God's image bearers! However, I can't say that until recently I loved many people *well* because I've had a sort of shotgun approach to relationships. I sprayed lots of people with pellets of affection but rarely lingered long enough or deep enough for true love. I was a fervent *liker* but a feeble *lover*.

Thankfully, that began to change three years ago. Not because I had an enlightening epiphany, but because I lost two people I wish I'd loved better. In the span of a few months I lost my stepfather, John Angel, who'd been my de facto dad since I was six years old. And I lost my best friend of fifteen years. I'd never lost a parent or a close friend before, and to say I wasn't a good loser is putting it mildly.

I grieved Dad Angel more for what could have been than for what was. From the outside, we looked like a happily blended family after he and mom got married. He was a successful school superintendent, principal, and regarded as a strong and effective leader by his colleagues. He was a very affectionate husband, often referring to mom as the love of his life and the most beautiful woman in the world. And he was a passionate outdoorsman—if there was just one bass in a big lake, he could hook it! Dad was also brilliant. He read voraciously, understood quantum physics, and could build *anything*. He built two big homes (one in North Carolina and one in Florida), state-of-the-art boats with teak consoles and cabinetry, and hand-carved, perfectly detailed duck decoys, to name a few.

I think the only thing Dad Angel wasn't good at was being a father. I believe he wanted to connect with us, he just didn't know how. He seemed much more comfortable in the role of boss than parent. He soberly monitored my food intake because he equated being overweight with low intellect and laziness; he refused to attend any of my volleyball games or tennis matches because he was concerned that women who participated in sports became lesbians; he didn't invest money in my college education because he thought most women just went to college to find a man, then got married and had babies, and never used their degree—so he considered my continuing education a "bad investment." Then, when I graduated from Troy University (where I'd received a volleyball scholarship) and decided to go into youth ministry, he said, "Yours is the biggest waste of a mind I've ever seen."

He wasn't hateful or malicious, he just wasn't emotionally connected to us. That is, until the very end of his life, when he was eighty-seven years old and the edges of his sharp mind were dulled by Alzheimer's disease and his logical defenses against Jesus had been trampled by the evangelistic zeal of my ten-year-old nephew, John Michael. Then my crotchety old daddy got softer and his emotional IQ went through puberty. Then he reached for my hand when he was conscious. Then he asked me questions about things that matter. Then he sang hymns I didn't know he'd memorized in childhood. Then he told me he loved me and I knew he meant it.

A week or so after Dad Angel died in 2010, I found a letter on my laptop that I'd written him six years earlier. We only talked about it once—when I asked him if he had any questions about it and he said with a characteristically sparse reply, "No." But mom told me he used to carry it in his back pocket and carefully unfold it and reread these words when he didn't think anyone was looking:

November 23, 2004

Dear Dad,

I'm writing this letter for two main reasons: first of all, I want to thank you for the positive influence you've had on me in several specific areas, and secondly, I want to share my heart with you in a way that spoken words have failed me.

I don't think I've ever really enumerated the things I admire about you . . . and the list is pretty long! You taught me to be an inquisitive, passionate student. I can remember asking you endless questions on that thirty-minute ride to and from Teague Middle School. And while I don't remember all the answers, I do remember your willingness to listen, the way you responded thoughtfully, and how you affirmed my curiosity in whatever subject I was currently interested in. Once I asked you how thread was made and you spent the longest time explaining the mechanics of looming and tensile strength! I grew up thinking I had unlimited mental potential partly because you acted like my questions were worthwhile and never patronized me. Thank you for engaging with me instead of turning up the radio or daydreaming about fishing!

This brings me to another thing I admire about you: your love of the outdoors. Even though I don't have the patience you have to sit in a hot boat waiting for a finicky bass to bite, I still love being outside! And I can still handle a rod and reel as a result of those casting lessons in the pool! Those long afternoons in the airboat with you on the St. John's River instilled in me a love for nature that continues to this day. I'm glad you took us camping more often than you took us to Disney. Thank you for sharing your favorite pastime with me.

And I've always admired your intellect. I've used the adjective "brilliant" to describe you many times. Not only did you respond to my questions, you also helped me learn how to think logically before I asked a question. I didn't always appreciate your Socrates "Answer a Question with a Question" method when I was growing up . . . because it wasn't as convenient as the "fill in the blank" method! But I read countless books and articles after you asked me what I thought instead of giving me a pat answer. And the fact that you continue to read and reason as an eighty-something-year-old retiree inspires me to never settle for mental mediocrity. Thank you for your example of intellectual energy.

. . . .

I also admire your work ethic. The sight of you fixing something in the house or swinging a hammer to build one of mom's "projects" was so common that I was always surprised when my friends' fathers couldn't build an armoire from scratch or had to call a plumber to fix a leak! I respected the fact that you presided over a big staff during the week as a "white collar" success, but still got your hands dirty on the weekends. You once told me that there wasn't anything I couldn't accomplish if I read the directions and was willing to work hard, and I've pretty much lived by that mantra. The only negative thing about emulating your work ethic is that I have two ruptured discs because I hate hiring someone else to do the heavy lifting! Thanks for modeling the value of elbow grease and hard work, Dad.

And finally, I'm thankful for your integrity. I clearly remember you taking the "high road" during the Superintendent Election and choosing to keep your mouth shut so as to not malign another candidate. I was so proud of you! I thought anyone who cast a vote for him was deluded and needed to know that "my dad" was the good guy! Thank you for tangibly living the mantra of "If you don't have anything nice to say, don't say anything at all" during that difficult season. You taught me that character is more important than the popular vote.

....

There are so many other things I respect about you, Dad . . . so many things that have left an indelible mark on my heart and life. But there is one thing I grieve about our relationship too, and that is we don't share the same view of God. One of my favorite authors, Dr. Francis Schaeffer, said once, "I may disagree with you, but I will die for your right to disagree with me."[2] I deeply respect his statement. I don't want to be one of those shrill Christians who harasses innocent bystanders and considers people who don't believe in God "projects" to beat over the head with a Bible or argue with. But I do want to share my beliefs as earnestly and clearly as I can. Especially with people I love. Therefore, I wanted to write about our contrasting philosophies of God in the hope that you would understand me more completely, and maybe even begin to see a different facet of who God is.

Secular humanism (which I think you would agree is the organized system of thought that most closely mirrors your own) asserts that human reasoning is sufficient and a relationship with "god" is merely a crutch for intellectual cripples (and maybe Southern republicans!). Secular humanists insist that we can create universal, ethical standards by which to regulate society, rather than using the "archaic, old-fashioned" biblical guidelines for human interaction and morality.

. . . .

But taking that line of thinking to a logical conclusion brings us to the reality that human reasoning is a very dangerous tool. Because it will always be handicapped by man's prejudice. For instance, the ethical "standards" Hitler advocated couldn't be condemned if behavior and morality were based solely on human reasoning and truth was considered relative. His views are valid in the context of secular humanism. Thus, the ideals of secular humanism don't stand up to serious scrutiny.

The philosophy that followed secular humanism was/is postmodernism, which you may have considered in recent years in light of your reading material. You've at least observed it in the culture at large. And you undoubtedly know that postmodernism isn't idealistic like secular humanism, nor is it passionate about persuading others to believe in a particular creed or value system. Rather, postmodernism is an apathetic way of thinking; practitioners are irreverent to anything sacred or authoritative. They're often characterized by boredom, cynicism, and skepticism.

The philosophy of postmodernism is completely indifferent to context, consistency, or continuity. It generally advocates total disregard for an object's history, meaning, or creation. That's why postmodernists consider Andy Warhol's replica of a Campbell's soup can to be as valuable artistically as Michelangelo's David or Leonardo da Vinci's Mona Lisa. *There is a denial of any standards by which we can judge something to be beautiful or good.*

And when it comes to God, postmodernism says that there is nothing transcendent. So even if one does believe in a supreme being who created the world—that "god" couldn't truly know us or understand us. Postmodernists believe there is no meta-narrative or divine "author" to give life meaning or the hope of eternal significance. Thus, there's no hope of human beings understanding one another because we don't have a larger story connecting us; we're all just fragmented, biological collections of cells.

My philosophy is markedly different from secular humanism or postmodernism. I believe in a transcendent God, who knows me and loves me! I believe in a supernatural realm that exists just as surely as the physical world we can experience with our senses. But I also understand your reticence to believe in the supernatural, Dad. Especially after you've spent the better part of your life as an educator, where common sense and rational thinking are the necessary tools of the trade. And admittedly, common sense and rational thinking are often absent in the emotive language of Christianity. That's probably why Sören Kierkegaard (a Danish philosopher from the 1800s, who's considered to be the father

....

of modern thinking) said you couldn't approach religion with reason, but by a "leap of faith."[3]

However, I respectfully disagree with Kierkegaard and most modern, postmodern, and post-postmodern philosophers, who insist there's a chasm between faith and logic. The God I've come to know is infinitely realistic as well as historically credible. Francis Schaeffer also wrote that Christianity is realistic because it says, "the world is marked with evil and man is truly guilty . . . it is poles apart from any form of optimistic humanism, but it also differs from nihilism, for nihilism, though it is correctly realistic, nevertheless can give neither a proper diagnosis nor the proper treatment for its own ills."[4] Atheistic philosophers from different schools of thought agree with the concept of evil in mankind and the futility of our natural life or "metaphysical lostness." What they can't agree on is the tangible existence of a supernatural God.

Schaeffer describes him as "The God Who is There"[5] and he is that to me, Dad. The God I'm in relationship with bears no resemblance to the caricature perpetuated in some congregations. He's not a cartoon deity—a Santa Claus who bestows blessings when we check off all the items on the "good" list, or a punitive celestial grouch who blasts us when we make a mistake.

He is the Creator of the physical universe that we

. . . .

can touch, taste, smell, and see. He's the one who put gills on bass so they could survive in a watery environment. He's the one who set the moon and stars in place and gave the earth the exact composition of oxygen, nitrogen, and the other things on the periodic table you'd still be able to name that support human life! And He's also the one who dispatched his supernatural son, Jesus, to earth in a suit of skin. To live a perfect life, in a human body, in actual time and space. The life (and ultimate death) of Jesus Christ isn't just recorded biblical history but was also recorded in Jewish, Greek, and Roman historical documents (not prone to bias or tampering).

This incarnate Jesus taught about knowing God personally, a concept that was very unpopular in religious Jewish circles where a select few had appointed themselves as the only liaisons to God. Jesus said God was accessible to everyone. Even to those who didn't have the money or political clout to fit into the organized religion of their culture. He was the very first person to encourage common people to call God "Abba"—the Hebrew word for "Daddy"—which was considered heretical and definitely threatened the current religious leaders' self-aggrandizing, manipulative theology, and money-making schemes.

Thus, those same "church leaders" plotted his death

via a bogus arrest and trial, unwittingly becoming pawns in God's divine plan to fulfill an ancient sacrificial system through the blood of Jesus. When he died on that Roman cross (a historical event we observe on "Good Friday"), Jesus figuratively, metaphorically, and literally redeemed mankind from this world—fractured by sin and self-absorption—into a right relationship with God.

Contrary to philosophies that claim man is inherently good, all you have to do is remember the spankings you gave as a principal to know we're not! We're separated from God because of real moral guilt. We're also separated from our "true selves" because we weren't created to live outside of a relationship with God. And in our natural state of egocentrism, we're also separated from true intimacy with other people. Basically, life without God is a pointless, unsatisfying, lonely existence that gets sadder the closer you get to physical death. Apart from faith in Jesus Christ and what he accomplished on the cross, we have no hope for real "soul" satisfaction or lasting joy.

But God created a way for us to be reunited with Him. He isn't a Sunday school fable or some philosophy drummed up by narrow-minded legalists who wanted a system to moderate human behavior. He is a knowable God. You just have to expand your thinking to include

. . . .

the supernatural . . . to realize that this world isn't our final resting place. G. K. Chesterton said it well: "We have come to the wrong star . . . That is what makes life at once so splendid and so strange. The true happiness is that we don't fit. We come from somewhere else. We have lost our way."[6]

My guess is that considering God to be "knowable" and Christianity to be rational or credible is still a stretch for you. Because not only do your intellectual presuppositions get in the way, but your personal experience with some confessing Christians—like mom, mom's family, and me—has been less than convincing. Instead of being shining examples of grace, mercy, and compassion, all too often we've been critical, demanding shrews!

One of my favorite philosophers, a brilliant French mathematician and theologian named Blaise Pascal, said, "God created man in his own image and then we returned the favor."[7] It's a sad reality that when God is viewed through the lens of human frailty, He appears to be less than impressive. I'm so sorry we've been barriers more than bridges when it comes to you believing in God's goodness.

Another one of my favorite philosophers and writers is C. S. Lewis, and he wrote a poem addressing the flaws in his "lens" that goes like this:

. . . .

All this is flashy rhetoric about loving you.

I never had a selfless thought since I was born.

I am mercenary and self-seeking through and through;

I want God, you, all friends, merely to serve my turn.

Peace, reassurance, pleasure, are the goals I seek,

I cannot crawl one inch outside my proper skin;

I talk of love—a scholar's parrot may talk Greek

But, self-imprisoned, always end where I begin.[8]

C. S. Lewis was a talented author, professor, and, according to most who knew him, a wonderful friend. Yet at his core, he honestly admits he was selfish. So am I. Not a day goes by that I don't think about myself, work to arrange things more to my liking, or try to make others like me. I'm most often a dim reflection of selfless love and genuine kindness toward others. I don't resemble Jesus the way I'm supposed to.

But I'm also the poster child for why people need

God. We're broken individuals, living in a broken world. We need help. Left to our own devices, we don't love well. We're like the teenage bully whose report card includes the comment, "Doesn't play well with others." Even the best of us need guidance, compassion, and sometimes, divine discipline.

We also need to believe in something beyond ourselves, beyond our own weakness and vanity, beyond the human condition. Something intrinsically good and true. And the only person who fits that description is God.

I'm closing this letter with something I wrote recently about the New Testament book of Hebrews. Hebrews was written to a group of ancient Christians facing horrible persecution—including martyrdom—and their pastor was encouraging them to have faith in God regardless of their situation. His hope for them to have peace even when they were facing physical death is similar to the hope I have that you'll find real peace through a relationship with God in the waning years of your life too, Dad.

My friend's eleven-year-old son, Greg, is a football fanatic. He plays in a youth league, watches ESPN religiously, keeps track of several teams' statistics, and attends every high school, college, and pro game he can. So you can imagine how excited Greg was when Nashville got our very own NFL team, the Tennessee Titans. He covered his walls with their pictures and begged for jerseys for his birthday and Christmas. His dad got them tickets for most of the home games and I got used to the sight of him in blue face paint. I thought he'd be a Smurf look-alike for good when the Titans made it to the Super Bowl! But then they had a so-so season and their halo started slipping.

As the losses mounted, Greg's football heroes faded to ignominy. The posters came down, playing cards were traded, and the blue jerseys were shoved to the back of the closet. His exuberant faith in his favorite team eroded during that difficult season. I had to bite my lip to keep from grinning when he soberly confided that he "just wasn't into the Titans" anymore.

Much like Greg, I think the Hebrews were becoming fair-weather fans. The difficulties they were facing dimmed their adoration for Jesus. They were tired of defeat and sick of being harassed; they wanted to win again. They became wistful about easier, more successful seasons with different coaches. They started peeling the poster of the great "Lion of Judah" off their walls and began rinsing off the paint of devotion. And that's when their mentor steps in to stop their slide toward faithlessness.

Ever been there? Have you ever wished for a different kind of "Coach," one who didn't demand a lifetime of selflessness and lugging crosses and blind faith?

I have. Every now and then, when I can't see around the corner of my circumstances or when I feel alone or misunderstood, I whine for a different kind of Messiah. One who would make all my messes disappear. Who'd answer my prayer for a husband and children with an immediate "Yes." Who'd make my closest friends interested listeners, conscientious encouragers, and fatter than me. Sometimes I wish our Hero of a Savior would make my life less hard.

Of course a Savior like that only exists in fairy tales and isn't actually very heroic. Because a Messiah who only served to grant our wishes would be akin to an overly indulgent mother who let her child eat all the candy he wanted, stay up as late as he liked, and never made him accept responsibility or obey authority. Pretty soon she's got a middle-aged man with no job, no friends, and no respect for her still living in his boyhood room and demanding Twinkies for lunch.

....

Jesus didn't die to make us happy. He's not some cartoonish character flitting around in a sparkly outfit and waving a magic wand. He's not Cinderella's godmother; He's the sovereign Son of the Most High God. And He sacrificed His life because that was the only way to reconcile sinners like us with that very same God. Jesus died so we could get to know our Heavenly Father. The dreams He fulfilled for us are much grander than the confines of our finite imaginations.

Hebrews reminds us of what we should look for in a champion. Because whether we look up to Martin Luther, Martin Luther King, Martin Scorsese, or Moses . . . they all have clay feet. They all make mistakes and tumble off pedestals. We have to keep our eyes on Jesus; He's the only One who deserves the distinction of hero.

Then I turned to see the voice that was speaking to me, and on turning I saw seven golden lampstands, and in the midst of the lampstands one like a son of man, clothed with a long robe and with a golden sash around his chest. The hairs of his head were white like wool, as white as snow. His eyes were like a flame of fire,

. . . .

his feet were like burnished bronze, refined in a furnace, and his voice was like the roar of many waters. In his right hand he held seven stars, from his mouth came a sharp two-edged sword, and his face was like the sun shining in full strength. When I saw him, I fell at his feet as though dead. But he laid his right hand on me saying, "Fear not, I am the first and the last, and the living one. I died, and behold I am alive forevermore, and I have the keys of Death and Hades." (Revelation 1:12–18)

Please forgive me if I've written anything that offended you, Dad. I debated sending this letter to you, but in the end felt compelled to. Because I love you very much . . . too much to withhold the most important thing in my life. Plus, my fear of offending you pales next to my fear of what will happen to you if you don't put your faith in Christ. It grieves me to think about your eternity because at this point, I believe you'll be separated from God—and us—forever.

And it's not just the state of your soul after death that worries me, your existence here on earth troubles me too. You've never seemed truly happy, peaceful, or content. A relationship with God isn't just a "Get Out of Hell Free" card; He also gives purpose and meaning

. . . .

to our natural lives. I'd love to see the last ten or twenty years you have left marked by peace, contentment, and joy . . . and I don't think that's possible without God.

So may I challenge you to really consider the claims of Christ? To ask questions. To ponder the historical reality of the life, death, and resurrection of Jesus. You're too smart to dismiss Jesus because of the behavior of a few hypocritical preachers and some selfish loved ones. And you're too smart to categorize Christianity as illogical or irrational without studying it systematically. God is big enough for your questions, Dad. I hope you respect your wife, children, and grandchildren—all of whom have put their faith in Jesus—enough to ask them.

Again, I love you very much. And I'll be glad to talk about any of this with you when I come home for Thanksgiving.

Yours,
Lisa

After rereading this rationally-based missive to my father, I had one thought: *I'm so much like him.* Which was an arresting thought because I always assumed my apple had fallen miles away from his proverbial tree. But when I got brave enough to look at my own reflection, I was stunned by the resemblance. Especially when it came to

....

relationships. I'm chattier than Dad ever was, so I'm more gifted at feigning deep feelings, but the real truth of the matter is I ran scared for most of my life. I was terrified of being hurt. I was afraid if I allowed myself to really love someone, they'd ultimately abandon me and I'd be left with a gaping, irreparable hole in my soul. Just like Dad, I typically kept my heart out of the line of fire.

I wish I'd been more committed to loving Dad *well*. I wish I'd peppered him with more questions. I wish I'd trusted and respected him enough when I got older to talk about the things he did and said that made me feel devalued. I wish I'd looked deeper into his eyes when I told him I loved him. But I didn't. I looked away. I let layer after layer of woundedness become a wall around my heart. I let fear kidnap the genuine affection I had for him as a bright-eyed second grader when he married mom and moved into our home.

I wish I'd trusted my Heavenly Father enough with my heart to risk it more for my stepfather. John might not have been capable of loving me back as big as I loved him in the beginning, but now I realize he was worth stretching myself for. I think most people are. *Love bigger. Fear smaller. Run headlong into the arms of Jesus every single day.* Whether you're dealing with a difficult dad, a towering cliff, or the death of a loved one, life has taught me those three aspects of overextension are joined at the hip.

7

THE GLORIOUS STRETCH
OF GRATITUDE

For many, it is difficult to accept that the
past has passed. Sometimes, it's so hard to
just leave it there, where it belongs.[1]

—*Craig Groeschel*

There are hard days, like one Friday last spring, when
I was in the Green Room at The Cove (also known
as The Billy Graham Training Center, which is
located in Asheville, North Carolina) pondering about
what an undeserved honor it was to be teaching at a retreat

there. *I mean, good night, most of my living heroes of the faith have spoken there before me: J. I. Packer, Ravi Zacharias, Anne Graham Lotz, Jim Cymbala, and of course, the legendary Billy Graham himself.* I found myself teary over the wonder of it all in the restroom while giving my hair one last blast of hairspray before taking the stage and thought: *Wow, this is such an anointed setting, even the air inside smells like pine trees!* Then it dawned on me that I'd just given my coiffure a heavy coating of Glade Air Freshener.

Then there are *hard* days, like February 7, 2013, when, on my thirty-second day in a row of being on the road, I received a phone call from mom while eating breakfast at the Holiday Inn in Redding, California, telling me that my Dad Harper had just passed away. Dad's death wasn't a surprise. He'd been struggling with cancer for about seven years and the doctor had told him he had approximately two months to live about ten months ago. Plus, I'd spent the week before with him and it was obvious his death was imminent. But still, I don't think your heart is ever truly prepared for news like that and when I ended the call, I felt my emotional knees buckle.

Several times over the last few months of Dad's life, my sister, Theresa, remarked, "The best thing Dad's ever done in his life is die." She didn't mean it in a cruel way, as in she was looking forward to his death. But she was recognizing that the closer he got to the grave, the sweeter he'd become. In fact, every time I talked to him over the past year or so, whether in person or on the phone, he cried while trying to explain how much he loved me. Until then, I'd never seen or heard him cry.

But Daddy also had a tendency to edit history in those conversations. He said things like, "Don't you worry about the future, Lisa. God gave me the money to send you to college when I didn't have two nickels to rub together, so you can trust that He will always provide for your needs." And, "I need you to know that you and your sister have always been what mattered most to me in life. I love you more than it's possible to love another person."

The problem I had in hearing his tender proclamations was they weren't exactly true. The only financial investment he made in my college education was giving me a coffee can full of change when I told him I didn't have enough money for books one semester. The rest of it was paid for by athletic scholarships and by me working two jobs every summer and delivering thousands of pounds of packages while working for UPS every Christmas break. And I couldn't help thinking that if I were what mattered *most* to him in life, he sure had a funny way of showing it, because he left me in alone in a bar when I was little,

....

where I was sexually molested while he was off philandering with one of the waitresses. A year or so later he left us for good to marry another woman with whom he'd been having an affair. Then, even though mom allowed him to have weekend visitation privileges, he often failed to show up when he promised and rarely bothered to remember our birthdays.

I absolutely *hated* feeling a resurgence of the resentment I'd worked so hard to wrestle to the ground in my twenties and thirties. But I couldn't deny its presence. I couldn't deny I was having a hard time with the incongruence between what Dad reminisced about and what really happened.

One of my favorite stories in the whole Bible is the following familiar tale Jesus told, which at first glance seems to be about a flagrant prodigal and his forgiving father.

> Once there was this man who had two sons. One day the younger son came to his father and said, "Father, eventually I'm going to inherit my share of your estate. Rather than waiting until you die, I want you to give me my share now." And so the father *liquidated assets and* divided them. A few days passed and this younger

son gathered all his wealth and set off on a journey to a distant land. Once there he wasted everything he owned on wild living. He was broke, a terrible famine struck that land, and he felt desperately hungry and in need. He got a job with one of the locals, who sent him into the fields to feed the pigs. The young man felt so miserably hungry that he wished he could eat the slop the pigs were eating. Nobody gave him anything.

So he had this moment of self-reflection: *"What am I doing here?* Back home, my father's hired servants have plenty of food. Why am I here starving to death? I'll get up and return to my father, and I'll say, 'Father, I have done wrong—wrong against God and against you. I have forfeited any right to be treated like your son, but I'm wondering if you'd treat me as one of your hired servants?'" So he got up and returned to his father. The father looked off in the distance and saw the young man returning. He felt compassion for his son and ran out to him, enfolded him in an embrace, and kissed him.

The son said, "Father, I have done a terrible wrong in God's sight and in your sight too. I have forfeited any right to be treated as your son."

But the father turned to his servants and said, "Quick! Bring the best robe we have and put it on him. Put a ring on his finger and shoes on his feet. Go get

....

the fattest calf and butcher it. Let's have a feast and celebrate because my son was dead and is alive again. He was lost and has been found." So they had this huge party.

Now the man's older son was still out in the fields working. He came home at the end of the day and heard music and dancing. He called one of the servants and asked what was going on. The servant said, "Your brother has returned, and your father has butchered the fattest calf to celebrate his safe return."

The older brother got really angry and refused to come inside, so his father came out and pleaded with him to join the celebration. But he argued back, "Listen, all these years I've worked hard for you. I've never disobeyed one of your orders. But how many times have you even given me a little goat to roast for a party with my friends? Not once! *This is not fair!* So this son of yours comes, this wasteful delinquent who has spent your hard-earned wealth on loose women, and what do you do? You butcher the fattest calf from our herd!"

The father replied, "My son, you are always with me, and all I have is yours. Isn't it right to join in the celebration and be happy? This is your brother we're talking about. He was dead and is alive again; he was lost and is found again!" (Luke 15:11–32 The Voice)

....

Author and pastor Tim Keller teaches that the parable of the prodigal son would be more aptly titled if it was called the parable of two lost sons because the point Jesus was making wasn't just about the rebellious baby brother and the undeserved forgiveness of his daddy. He brings to light a more subtle moral of this story that he describes as "elder-brother lostness" in his book *The Prodigal God*:

> We see that the elder brother "became angry." All of his words are dripping with resentment. The first sign you have an elder-brother spirit is that when your life doesn't go as you want, you aren't just sorrowful but deeply anger and bitter. Elder brothers believe that if they live a good life, they should get a good life, that God owes them a smooth road if they try very hard to live up to standards.[2]

Ouch. Sometimes the truth stings like a wasp on steroids.

Rereading *The Prodigal God* and then reading renowned psychological researcher Dr. Brené Brown's new book, *Daring Greatly*, helped me reach past my own disappointment and really embrace Dad in his last days. In *Daring Greatly* she writes:

> When I asked people who had survived tragedy how we can cultivate and show more compassion for people who are suffering, the answer was always the same: Don't shrink away from the joy of your child because I've lost mine. Don't take what you have for granted—celebrate it. Don't apologize for what you have. Be grateful for it and share your gratitude with others. Are your parents healthy? Be thrilled. Let them know how much they mean to you. *When you honor what you have, you're honoring what I've lost.*[3]

She goes on to emphasize the importance of not squandering joy:

> We can't prepare for tragedy and loss. When we turn every opportunity to feel joy into a test drive for despair, we actually diminish our resilience. Yes, softening into joy is uncomfortable. Yes, it's scary. Yes, it's vulnerable. *But every time we allow ourselves to lean into joy and give in to those moments, we build resilience and we cultivate hope.* The joy becomes part of who we are, and when bad things happen—and they do happen—we are stronger.[4]

God's Spirit used those words to prompt me to practice gratitude in order to bridge the gap between my disappointment with Dad and my desire to embrace and engage him as much as possible while he was still here to love. And when I extended my neck (better yet, *overextended* it, in light of the title of this book) far enough outside my shell of self-protection and pride, I could see memories with Dad that I was very, very thankful for. Like the time he surprised Theresa and me with a coming-home party one Christmas.

I was twenty-four years old at the time and was on staff with a youth ministry in Nashville, which meant I had a million retreat T-shirts but very little money! Therefore I couldn't afford to fly home for the holidays, so I called my sister who lives in Birmingham, Alabama, and asked if she'd be willing to take a road trip to Florida with me. I gave my best sales pitch about what an adventure it'd be—kind of like the *Planes, Trains and Automobiles* movie with John Candy and Steve Martin, except without the flatulence parts.

Surprisingly, she agreed.

While planning our itinerary, we decided we'd go to Dad's house first because, while he doesn't talk much, he always found a way to express his displeasure over how we spent more time with mom than we did with him when we came to Florida. So we called him to explain that we were coming to hang out with him before we went home to be with mom and we told him the day and approximate time of our arrival. We could only hope he was pleased by our decision because, per usual, he didn't say much in response. We called him again, early in the morning just before leaving Birmingham, to let him know we were on the road and should be pulling into his driveway around six o'clock that night (this was during the period of ancient history when cell phones were bigger than a moose head and very expensive, so we didn't have one to touch base with him while en route).

About nine hours, several Diet Cokes and orders of French fries later, we turned the corner into Dad's neighborhood. However, we had to park a block away from his house because there were so many cars perched on either side of the road and we could see from the distance that even Dad's driveway was full. Theresa and I thought the Longwood Police Department (which is located near his house) must be having their annual Christmas party, wherein one of the officers plays Santa and they hand out presents to needy kids living in the area.

But as we began walking toward Dad's place, we realized that wasn't the case, because a family with children was walking beside us and they passed the station and kept walking toward Dad's house. That's when we noticed there were lots of people milling around

....

in Dad's yard, along with one of those huge grills with smoke billowing up—like the ones concession stands cook hot dogs and hamburgers on at the ballpark in the summer. I thought, *Gosh, I know Dad's not much of a talker, but it would've been nice if he told us he'd moved.* It didn't cross my mind that Dad was the one throwing the barbecue because he wasn't really a party-in-the-yard kind of guy.

Then I spotted him standing near the grill, holding a giant metal spatula, wearing an apron and a grin. Theresa and I were dumbfounded when he shouted something like, "Here they are!" and fifty or so people gathered around us and started clapping. Several of whom confided in the minutes afterward that they were expecting us to be much, much younger because Dad had invited his whole Sunday school class to the shindig with the very atypical, emotionally-charged announcement: "My little girls are finally coming home. Please come over and help me celebrate." So they thought he must be at the end of a protracted, acrimonious custody battle and Theresa and I were children.

As I chose to focus on that one amazing memory—our very own the-prodigals-have-returned-home kind of soiree—in the months prior to Dad's death, my soul stretched beyond the good things that *weren't* to the good things that *were*. I could then let myself marinate in the memories of other wonderful times spent with him, like when he patiently taught me to shoot a pistol and carefully placed egg after egg in the crook of a tree until I was able to hit them spot on. Or the time when I was the only girl included in a deer-hunting party. And then when I was also the only one with a clear shot at a big, beautiful buck and I fired my shotgun in the air—so he could escape into the woods instead of becoming filets in the freezer—Dad didn't reprimand me even though his camouflage-clad buddies were furious that I'd "ruined" the day. Or the time he let me rescue the sickly runt of a pig litter by nursing "Porky" back to health with a baby bottle and then keeping him in a dog bed on the porch for a year. Or when he drove me to visit a gorgeous horse named Gypsy at a neighbor's farm for the umpteenth time, watched me feed her yet another apple, and then said brusquely, "Come on and help me load her up on the trailer because I bought her for you."

Despite his prolonged absences, I realized we were never very far from his mind. Despite his rough demeanor, there was always a morsel of tenderness reserved for us. And while almost every conversation I had with him that lasted more than a few minutes involved him jabbing his finger at me and gruffly preaching about something I *ought to be doing*, what he really wanted to do, but just didn't have the tools to, was wrap his arms around me and say, "I love you. You are what matters most to me."

Practicing gratitude for what *was* good opened the floodgates to more sweeter times with Dad during the final chapter of his life than I'd dreamed possible.

Throughout the last few days he was coherent, it felt totally natural to lie in bed next to him and sing hymns or read to him from his Bible, even though I'd never had the opportunity or inclination to recline beside my father in the forty-seven years prior to that. I wanted to brush his hair back from his forehead and gently rub ice chips on his lips even though I couldn't remember ever touching his face before. And instead of rolling my eyes inwardly when he whispered, "No man has ever loved his children more than I've loved you and Theresa," God graciously created an opening wide enough in my heart to receive the "meant to" behind his grand claim.

In my experience, there's a ditch on either side of the road of life that people tend to get stuck in when they've suffered painful, traumatic, or deeply disappointing events. One ditch is that of *minimizing their emotional*

wounds and the other is *stage-lighting them*. I've spun my wheels in both. I've tried to minimize my wounds by shoving them shamefully into the darkest corner of my heart and refusing to let someone safe examine the damage and put proverbial Neosporin on the ones that were still oozing. And I've stage-lit my wounds by framing them with inspirational speeches that vilified Dad and cast me as the hobbling hero. Several times I found myself in mud up to my armpits before I even realized I was in a ditch.

Thankfully, the Holy Spirit motors around in a big four-wheel-drive truck with a winch. After He pulls me out, He leaves notes like this on my windshield:

Know this: the Eternal One Himself is the True God. He is the One who made us; we have not made ourselves; we are His people, like sheep *grazing* in His fields. Go through His gates, giving thanks; walk through His courts, giving praise. Offer Him your gratitude and praise His *holy* name. Because the Eternal is good, His loyal love *and mercy* will never end, and His truth will last throughout all generations. (Psalm 100:3–5 THE VOICE)

This is the day that the LORD has made; let us rejoice and be glad in it. (Psalm 118:24)

....

And give thanks for everything to God the Father in the name of our Lord Jesus Christ. (Ephesians 5:20 NLT)

Do not be anxious about anything, but in every situation, by prayer and petition, with thanksgiving, present your requests to God. And the peace of God, which transcends all understanding, will guard your hearts and your minds in Christ Jesus. (Philippians 4:6–7 NIV)

Let the peace of Christ rule in your hearts, since as members of one body you were called to peace. And be thankful. Let the message of Christ dwell among you richly as you teach and admonish one another with all wisdom through psalms, hymns, and songs from the Spirit, singing to God with gratitude in your hearts. And whatever you do, whether in word or deed, do it all in the name of the Lord Jesus, giving thanks to God the Father through him. (Colossians 3:15–17 NIV)

As a former, frequent ditch dweller, I'm finally learning to keep my heart in the middle of the road. And I'm finding the ride is so much smoother when it's paved with thanksgiving.

....

My road manager, Sharon, and I have come up with a simple game when we're traveling for when one of us notices that the other is especially grumpy or negative. We call it the "Stop and Give Me Ten" game, and I assure you that in spite of the title, it has nothing to do with push-ups. (If I attempted ten push-ups in a row in my current out-of-shape state, I might break my nose when collapsing to the floor.) The "ten" in the title refers to all the fingers on two hands worth of things we're grateful for.

For instance, recently after a long day of delayed flights we got to our destination airport only to discover that the car rental company had given away the SUV Sharon had confirmed with a credit card and only had compact cars left. So after breaking two nails trying to cram all of our luggage and several heavy cases of books into the petite-mobile, I climbed into the passenger's seat with a huff. Then I began to complain about all the inconveniences—the delays, disgusting airport food, tiny seats, etc.—that we'd had to endure in the span of eight hours.

After listening to my whiney chorus for a while, she turned to face me and commanded in her best impression of a Master Army Sergeant: "*STOP AND GIVE ME TEN!*" So I stopped, partly because she was driving in Dallas traffic and I was afraid she was going to rear-end the car in front of us, and partly because I'd been on a really good griping roll! But then I submitted, held my hands up, and raised all ten fingers in quick succession:

I'm thankful our flights were only delayed and not canceled.

I'm thankful we're in a car instead of on foot.

I'm thankful I make enough money on the road to pay my mortgage.

I'm thankful I get to see women launch themselves into the arms of Jesus for the first time almost every weekend.

I'm thankful I got to make it home in time to be with Dad one last time before he passed away.

I'm thankful he and mom forgave each other and developed such a sweet friendship before he died.

I'm thankful I have family and friends who've experienced my long list of shortcomings and yet still love me.

I'm thankful God is so strong when I'm being such a weenie baby.

I'm thankful He's slow to anger and rich in compassion.

I'm thankful we're staying at a decent hotel tonight.

And it's amazing how just thirty-six seconds of practicing gratitude totally changed my mood. I went from Eeyore to Tigger in less than a minute.

....

I know it's a much more difficult thing to practice gratitude when your husband walks away, your baby dies, your cancer returns, or your company is downsized and you find yourself out of a job. But I promise it still works. Granted, it's more of a stretch, but extending past the pain of life to reach for the joy God promises is so very, very worth it.

P.S. One of the last requests my dad made before he went to his eternal home, when he barely had enough strength to speak, was to ask us to help him change into clean pajamas, his nice robe, and a pair of slippers. When the hospice nurse asked him why (because by that point completely changing his clothes was going to be quite an ordeal and physically painful for him), he furrowed his brows and croaked, "Because I'm about to be dancing on streets of gold and I don't want to show up barefoot and half-dressed!"

8

THE SWEETNESS OF
A SECOND WIND

If your Nerve, deny you—Go above your Nerve.[1]

—*Emily Dickinson*

T hree weeks after the adoption of Anna Price fell through, I had to attend a training workshop for the Women of Faith speaking team in Dallas. And while I was looking forward to being with my friends— or the Sisterhood of the Traveling Spanx, which is what I like to call our Women of Faith tribe—my heart was still too heavy to be very excited about spending the next three days giving extemporaneous speeches in front of professional speaking coaches who would then dissect our performances and give us pointers about how to become more effective communicators.

I smiled and acted polite and friendly at the reception the first night, but all I really wanted to do was blow off the coaching sessions, hole up in my hotel room, order room service, and watch romantic comedies like *Sleepless in Seattle*. The scene when Tom Hanks/Sam and his precocious son, Jonah, walk back out on the deck at the top of the Empire State Building to retrieve Jonah's backpack only to find Meg Ryan/Annie standing there holding it along with his teddy bear always slays me. Then after Tom/Sam and Meg/Annie stare longingly into each other's eyes and recognize they're meant to be together, he extends his hand toward her and says, "Shall we?" And she puts her hand in his and the music swells . . . well, that's enough heartwarming goo to keep me going for a while.

In fact, if that soundtrack played daily in the background of my life, I'm pretty sure I'd meet *my* soul mate and recover the metabolism I had in high school.

Well, anyway, since the top brass at Women of Faith had paid big bucks for us to enhance our gabbing skills, I decided blowing off the sessions wasn't an option. I did, however, choose to sit next to Sheila Walsh (who's one of my dearest friends and the second big sister God intended me to have if the Fall hadn't intervened, causing her to be born to a calm woman named Elizabeth in Scotland instead of to a chatty one in Florida named Patti) because I knew she was safe and was almost as heartbroken as I was over Anna Price, whom she and her husband, Barry, had started referring to as their niece.

Midway through the second lecture on "How to Prepare a Persuasive SCORRE (Subject, Central Theme, Objective, Rationale, Resources, Evaluation) Speech," Sheila and I were struck simultaneously by an acute case of ADD and began whispering about what had happened since we'd last seen each other (we tend to be naughty like that when sitting side by side).

She told me that she'd been in Cincinnati on Saturday, just two days before the workshop, and was supposed to give an inspirational talk to an auditorium full of Women of Faith group leaders. But right before she took the stage, the sound guy played an unedited video clip about the new "different and deeper" vision at Women of Faith, which still included a message from me talking enthusiastically about my upcoming adoption of Anna Price and how I couldn't wait to be her mother. Sheila said she was so thrown by the clip that she began weeping and couldn't compose herself for several minutes, which of course took the "inspi" right out of the inspirational message they'd asked her to share. And we both got teary all over again.

Dear Ken Davis, who was leading the workshop, was obviously a little distracted by our private whispering/mourning huddle, because right about the time we both started digging in our purses for Kleenex, he encouraged the class to take a ten-minute break. Sheila headed directly for the bathroom because she wasn't wearing waterproof mascara and, thus, looked like a raccoon. But since I was wearing the waterproof, albeit clumpy kind, I headed out into the hotel lobby to check the voice mails on my cell phone.

Three or four minutes later, Sheila walked back toward me looking more like a model and less like a rodent, to find me standing straight as a board, cell phone glued to my left ear, with fresh tears streaming down my face. Her big sister protective gene must've kicked in at that moment because she gestured to my phone with an expression of concern as if she wanted to find out what the monster on the other end was saying that was causing me to cry when I was already in such a fragile state. So I nodded my head back and forth vigorously to let her know it wasn't a "mean" call (you can probably tell by now that charades are one of my favorite pastimes), then pointed to the phone and mouthed widely, *It's about another BA-BY.*

And it was. It was Michelle Smalling (who also works

with the 147 Million Orphans organization) calling to tell me they'd just returned from Haiti where they met a very sick two-and-a-half-year-old little girl named Missy in a remote village whose mother had just died of AIDS. Michelle said that she didn't want to pressure me because she knew I'd just lost Anna Price, but if they couldn't find someone quickly who was willing to adopt her, Missy would probably die because she had contracted HIV from her mama and nobody knew her paternity, so there was no father to help. Therefore, she would likely be placed in an overcrowded, state-run orphanage for children with special needs where the life-expectancy rate is grim.

Michelle said she understood if I needed a day or two to pray about adopting her because it would be a life-changing choice. I told her that wasn't necessary because I'd been praying about a decision like this for almost thirty years, so I already knew what God wanted me to do. I'd been in jump-school for a really long time. I said, "I'd love to adopt Missy, Michelle." And at ten o'clock in the morning on April 16, 2012, I proceeded to leap off the highest cliff of my life. I felt pretty darn brave while I was sailing through the air . . . until about a week later when I belly flopped with a resounding and painful *thwack* into the dark waters below.

Within a week, I'd booked a flight for my first trip to Haiti and my social worker was amending my home study and adoption profile to include a child with special needs. She explained that the state of Tennessee requires a "positive parent" to receive extensive training on HIV so they knew what they were getting into and would be at least be cognitively prepared for the inevitable medical challenges that lay ahead. So I bought all the books required and signed up for online classes and thought, *This shouldn't be too complicated. I mean, Magic Johnson played professional basketball with HIV, so how bad can it be?*

Sometimes I'm flabbergasted by my own foolishness.

HIV is the human immunodeficiency virus. It is the virus that can lead to acquired immune deficiency syndrome, or AIDS. The Centers for Disease Control (CDC) estimates that about 56,000 people in the United States contracted HIV in 2006.

There are two types of HIV, HIV-1 and HIV-2. In the United States, unless otherwise noted, the term "HIV" primarily refers to HIV-1.

Both types of HIV damage a person's body by destroying specific blood cells, called CD4+ T cells, which are crucial to helping the body fight diseases.

Within a few weeks of being infected with HIV, some people develop flu-like symptoms that last for a week or two, but others have no symptoms at all. People living with HIV may appear and feel healthy for several years. However, even if they feel healthy, HIV is still affecting their bodies. All people with HIV should be seen on a regular basis by a health care provider experienced with treating HIV infection. Many people with HIV, including those who feel healthy, can benefit greatly from current medications used to treat HIV infection. These medications can limit or slow down the destruction of the immune system, improve the health of people living with HIV, and may reduce their ability to transmit HIV. Untreated early HIV infection is also associated with many diseases including cardiovascular disease, kidney disease, liver disease, and cancer. Support services are also available to many people with HIV. These services can help people cope with their diagnosis, reduce risk behavior, and find needed services.[2]

Just one click of my mouse had caused my stomach to hide behind my intestines with dread. *Yikes, that "People living with HIV may appear and feel healthy for several years . . . However, even if they feel healthy, HIV is still affecting their bodies" bit sounds pretty ominous.* Oh baby, little did I know at that point.

Six and a half weeks later I was on a flight from Miami

. . . .

bound for Port-au-Prince with the whole 147 Million Orphans team: Suzanne Mayernick, Gwen Oatsvall, Michelle Smalling, and Jan Eberle. I studied Creole the whole way, hoping that I'd be able to communicate a little with Missy when I met her. When we landed two hours later, the few Creole phrases I'd memorized so fastidiously were instantly vaporized in the heat. Actually the word *heat* doesn't do summer temperatures in Haiti justice because, being from the Southeast, I've thrown that word around my whole life. The earthquake-ravaged environment we entered was more like a super-loud oven . . . on broil. The kind of crazy hot that makes a grown woman make promises to Jesus about becoming a missionary in Africa if He'll just make a glass of iced water miraculously appear in her hot little hands. Of course, I've just repeated an oath someone else told me *she* made. Or being hyperbolic. I really can't remember which because, like I said, every rational thought in my head had been vaporized by that point.

After melting our way through customs and fighting off aggressive Haitian "porters" who were trying to grab our bags so as to get a tip, we were finally led to a diesel-belching school bus—sans air-conditioning—for a bone-jarring, two-and-a-half hour ride to Neply, the village Missy lives in. Neply is also where My Life Speaks is located—a wonderful faith-based organization focused on caring for children with special needs (who are often considered "throw-away" kids in impoverished countries like Haiti) and sharing the love of Jesus with the entire community around them through a feeding program, English classes, Bible studies, and soccer clinics.

But just as sure as my makeup melted off in the Port-au-Prince airport, so did the hassle of traveling to Neply melt the moment Fifi (Missy's neighbor who, along with her maternal grandmother, are the two women who've been taking care of her since her mom died) approached me, placed this petite, wide-eyed toddler in my arms, and said to her, "Blan mama. Blan mama." Meaning that I was the new white mother they'd been telling her about. Of course she began to whimper, so I tried to explain to Fifi that I probably shouldn't hold her right away; we needed to take it slow so Missy wouldn't be afraid.

However, Fifi only speaks five words of English: *I love you* and *Praise Jesus*. She kept repeating the latter over and over while beaming at me with a radiant, one-front-toothed smile (which I've absolutely adored since that first meeting). She also kept her arms crossed and refused to take Missy back. So I did the only thing I knew to do and that was flip Missy around so that I was cradling her back against my chest and she could face Fifi. Then I started to croon softly in her ear, "Shush, Fifi's right there, baby. Fifi's right there. It's okay. It's okay. Shush." Right then and there I felt my heart climb out of my body and curl around that baby. I knew I was magnificently ruined.

A few minutes later, after Missy seemed more relaxed and I was rocking her back and forth in my arms, Suzanne walked over and exclaimed, "She is such a cutie-pie! Have you checked her teeth yet?" I told her I hadn't even thought of checking her teeth. At which point Suzanne (who's more than experienced with sick orphans since a doctor in Uganda discouraged her from taking her now seven-year-old daughter Josie Love back to the States when she was a toddler, given the fact that her white blood cell count was almost non-existent due to the lack of treatment for her HIV; plus the fact that she had a known history of tuberculosis, as well as probably being infected with cholera and malaria meant that, in the doctor's opinion, Josie Love would surely die on the plane before they even landed back in Nashville) tickled her chin and got Missy to open her mouth to reveal uneven rows of tiny, brown nubs. A little closer inspection led to the identification of a host of other problems including: severe malnutrition, hair loss, a herniated belly button, some kind of skin virus, growths on her eyelids, and a deep, rheumy cough which is a sure sign of tuberculosis among children who are infected with HIV.

Suzanne said, "Oh Lisa, she's much sicker than we thought." At which point my heart and my mind drew swords and began to duke it out.

....

How in the world can I take care of a child this sick when I'm single with no family living nearby, and I'm on the road all the time?

JUST LOVE HER.

How will I pay for all the surgeries she needs if my health care plan won't cover them?

JUST LOVE HER.

Goodness gracious, what in the world am I going to do about her teeth?

JUST LOVE HER.

What if all the dentists I know refuse to treat her because surely the kind of extensive work she needs will cause bleeding, which would put them at risk for contracting HIV too?

JUST LOVE HER.

Why didn't I just adopt a domestic baby from a nice, clean adoption agency in America?

JUST LOVE HER.

Why don't I just adopt another dog from the Humane Society and call it quits?

JUST LOVE HER.

When I was in the process of adopting Anna Price, I met several couples who were initially ready and willing to adopt a crack baby, but then backed out when the realization of the myriad of problems a child born to a drug-addicted mother will likely have sunk in. And I'm embarrassed to admit it now, but I judged them pretty harshly. I thought to myself, *Good night, don't you two have HEARTS? Yeah, we're probably going to be sleep-deprived for a few months* (crack babies are notorious for being difficult to console in the first few months of life, much like a baby with acute colic). *And our kids might not make the honor roll because they'll probably have ADD or ADHD, but surely you aren't more concerned about award ceremonies and SAT scores than you are about A. CHILD'S. LIFE! I mean, COME ON! Why can't you just buck up, grow some compassion, and quit being such self-centered suburbanites?*

I didn't think I could ever be like them . . . until I was. Until I wasn't sure I could chew what I'd bitten off either.

Later that night, after I'd spent several hours with Missy, the girls and I were sitting up in our sweat-soaked bunk beds talking, because it's difficult to sleep inside a sauna. Gwen told harrowing tales of adopting internationally. Like when she showed up at the orphanage in China where she and her husband adopted their second little girl, Maggie. They discovered that, unlike the documents they'd received about Maggie's medical condition, which stated that she had "mild hair loss," she actually had a flap of skin covering a hole in her head though which Gwen could see her brain pulsing because doctors had removed a piece of her skull and had no way to replace it.

Furthermore, the life-saving surgeries that were performed on Maggie in China were done in a hospital that couldn't afford anesthesia, so that poor little punkin' had endured barbaric, invasive procedures without the benefit of being unconscious. Needless to say, she didn't like to be touched and screamed at an ear-splitting pitch the entire eighteen-hour flight back to Tennessee. At which point in her narrative, Gwen paused, turned toward me and asked, "So you know what I did?" I guessed, "Got drunk on a bunch of those little liquor bottles?" And she said, "Nope. I left her in my friend's lap (a woman who Gwen was hoping would become a Christian when she saw the parallels between the gospel and the process of adopting an orphan; she hasn't yet become a Christian and may still be in therapy!), locked myself in the lavatory, and sobbed for four hours."

She went on to proclaim passionately, "Any idiot who tries to sugarcoat adoption is a liar!" Suzanne and Michelle chimed in with enthusiastic agreement and described how adoption was by far the hardest thing they'd ever done in their lives. Then one of them said sincerely, "But it's so worth it. Plus, since the Bible commands us to take care of widows and orphans (James 1:27 says, "Religion that God our Father accepts as pure and faultless is this:

to look after orphans and widows in their distress and to keep oneself from being polluted by the world." NIV), if you have even an inkling of inclination toward adoption, how can you *not?*"

HOW. COULD. I. NOT? has echoed in my heart a million times since that first night in Neply. It's the chorus I sing when my head threatens to stage a coup and take over my heart. It's the phrase that coaxes me down off the ledge of *how*, *what*, and *why*.

I was leading a small group Bible study at The Next Door last summer when one of my girls (who's one of my absolute favorites) sighed loudly and interrupted the lesson by blurting out, "I sure do miss taking communion. I haven't taken communion in *YEARS!*" I closed my Bible and said, "Why haven't you had communion in so long, Melinda? They celebrate it at least once a month in the prison chapel."

At that time Melinda had only been a resident at The Next Door for a few weeks and prior to that she'd been incarcerated at the Tennessee Prison for Women for six years on charges of possession, possession with intent to sell, and being an accomplice in an armed robbery because she was driving the getaway car. So she should've had ample opportunity to celebrate communion while she was behind bars.

She slumped further back into the folding chair, harrumphed, sheepishly shrugged her shoulders, and then confessed, "'Cause I was usually in solitary confinement for fightin' so I wasn't allowed to go to chapel most times." I said, "Well, cutie, we can celebrate communion right here, right now, because the sacraments are just an outward symbol of what Jesus did for us on the Cross." Her eyes widened and she exclaimed, "Lisa, we caint have no communion because we ain't got no bread or grape juice!" I explained evenly, "Honey, there's a Pepsi bottle with some soda still in it on the desk behind you—that can symbolize the blood of Christ just like grape juice. And I've got some Ricola cough drops in my purse, which we can use to represent the body of Christ, the way we do with bread or crackers. Plus, they'll last longer and give us more time to think about how Jesus must really, really love us to allow His body to be broken like that."

Melinda's eyes widened further with alarm and she cried indignantly, "Lisa, we CAINT drink that Pepsi because we don't even know whose it is!" I replied teasingly, "Oh, good night, Melinda, you were an IV drug user for *years*! What's the big deal about drinking someone else's coke?" She eventually relented to my rationale and the other three girls in our circle said they wanted to have communion too, so I read this passage from Mark:

> While they were eating, Jesus took some bread and thanked God for it and broke it. Then he gave it to his followers and said, "Take it; this is my body."
>
> Then Jesus took a cup and thanked God for it and gave it to the followers, and they all drank from the cup.
>
> Then Jesus said, "This is my blood which is the new agreement that God makes with his people. This blood is poured out for many. I tell you the truth, I will not drink of this fruit of the vine again until that day when I drink it new in the kingdom of God." (Mark 14:22–25 NCV)

Then we each carefully poured a little warm Pepsi into the bottle cap and passed it to the person on our left saying, "This Pepsi represents the blood of Jesus, which He shed for you because He thinks you're worth it." After all five of us had sipped a capful of Pepsi, we passed a cough drop to the person on our left and said, "This Ricola represents the body of Jesus, which He broke for you because He thinks you're worth it." And when I looked around at those four precious recovering addicts sucking earnestly on lemon-flavored candies, tears began streaming down my face.

I thought, *I'll probably get a lecture about trivializing the sacraments if my seminary professors ever find out I did this, but it'll be worth it because I think these girls understand the gospel more in this moment than they ever have before.* And I'm pretty sure I did too.

How could I not?

9

LEARNING TO LET
WHATEVER WILL BE, BE

"Brennan, you don't need any more insights into the
faith," he observed. "You've got enough insights to
last you three hundred years. The most urgent need
in your life is to trust what you have received."[1]

—*Brennan Manning*

t's 6:20 a.m. on Monday, March 25, 2013, and I'm on my
way to Haiti for the second time. But first I have to trek to
Miami on this packed American Airlines jet full of people
who are conspiring to drive me bananas. The man behind me
is obviously the leader of the let's-put-Lisa-in-a-padded-cell

gang, as evidenced by the way he's enthusiastically pummeling my seatback. Or perhaps he's just starring in a documentary about causing mayhem on planes. Ah yes, I think I just saw the flash of his buddy's cell phone camera after he jarred me hard enough to slosh my thimble full of cran-apple juice all over my lap.

Meanwhile, the couple sitting next to me has not stopped making out since we taxied to the runway in Nashville. When the boyfriend, or husband, or very frisky man (whatever the case may be) in the window seat first turned toward the jittery girl to my left and kissed her, I thought he was just being solicitous because she was obviously afraid of flying. A little overt affection in that context seemed wholly appropriate to me.

But the consoling didn't stop there. Oh no, we're well into our flight plan now and the groping and slurping sounds are beginning to gross me out. Plus, she keeps bumping me in the throes of passion, which causes my cran-apple juice to tip over again. Between her and the boxer behind me, I'm going to look like I need Depends by the time we get to Miami.

Not that anyone will have time to notice because I've only got forty minutes to make the connecting flight to Port-au-Prince. My plan is to hustle off this plane as fast as possible when we get to the gate (I'm more than prepared to use my carry-on like a snow plow to shove pokey people aside) and then jog to the departing gate. I even remembered to wear running shoes this morning as part of my traveling ensemble.

I'm not usually that intentional about my flying attire, especially when I have to leave the house at four a.m., but I've been a little anxious about this particular trip. Because I'm going to Port-au-Prince for a meeting with the US Embassy and Haitian Immigration to file formal petitions to adopt Missy. And while I've been praying this day would come since I committed to adopt that little peanut on April 16, 2012, now that the official ball is rolling faster I'm kind of nervous.

First of all, I'm by myself. You know the pictures of adoptive families traveling to foreign countries on the adoption brochures? The ones with some super-cute, blond, thirty-ish woman and her affable, doting, I-played-college-football-before-my-hair-started-thinning husband with dimples? Sometimes their parents or in-laws are even part of the photogenic ensemble, complete with gorgeous silver hair and matching cardigans. Well, I don't look anything like that today. Nope, I'm just a forty-nine-year-old chick with gray roots and a backpack crammed full of enough candy and LeapFrog learning toys to delight and educate an army of toddlers.

The last time I navigated a third-world airport by myself, a giant bully of a man wrenched my carry-on bag

out of my hands and ran in the other direction right outside of the so-called security line. I yelled for help but all
the uniformed guys standing around watching the heist
just shrugged their shoulders and lifted their hands palms
up as if to say, *We're so sorry our second cousin with whom
we're in cahoots ran off with your belongings and your pass-
port. But our job description explicitly states that we must
remain sprawled here sipping orange soda when American
women get robbed.* I had to chase the shoplifter down
myself and get into a bit of a scuffle and eventually bribe
him with twenty-five dollars before he relinquished his
grip on my suitcase. Mind you, a similar shakedown happened to me at LAX, so I suppose I shouldn't limit my
unease to third-world airports.

I'm also a little worried about what some call the
"charming, laid-back" aspect of Caribbean culture. Based
on my last trip to Haiti, that means most things happen
approximately three to four hours later than planned.
Scheduled appointments, like flight arrivals or shuttle
pick-ups, are actually more of a suggestion than a commitment. That didn't trouble me when it simply meant
they hadn't yet killed the chicken we ordered for dinner.
I'm totally fine when it comes to going into a restaurant at
eight thirty p.m. and not coming out until midnight. No
big deal. I could stand to miss a meal anyway.

However, based on the e-mails I've received from the

US Embassy, several Haitian government entities are not quite so flexible. In fact, they made it sound like if I don't show up at the exact time they've assigned for me to be there, Missy's adoption will be in jeopardy and I'll be flogged in the town square!

One of my best friends in elementary school was a girl named Becky. It's mostly with fondness that I remember her because Becky taught me how to play pool. Which came in handy at Greek socials in college because every fraternity house on campus had a pool table and I always felt like popping those balls confidently in the correct position in the wooden triangle thingy, smoothly chalking my cue stick, and then crushing the equilateral triangle of orbs, sending them flying across the felt upped my flirting ante (by the way, I have no idea what an *ante* is, but I've always heard it used in association with *upped*). Becky also taught me about the birds and the bees. This was another good thing to know at nine because by then I'd heard scary rumors about how babies were made. Although, when Becky explained just how grotesque and acrobatic the ritual was, I couldn't help thinking that my mom and dad must love us a *lot* to endure that nasty mess THREE WHOLE TIMES.

But Becky also taught me what it looks like when daughters can't stand their mothers. I never quite figured out why she held her mother in such contempt. She always seemed like such a nice lady to me, what with her auburn beehive, wood-paneled station wagon, and pantry stocked with Little Debbie treats (a stark and glorious contrast to the way my mom always pointed to the orange and tangerine trees in the backyard when I asked for a snack and said, "There's more than you can eat right there!"). Maybe Becky's mom was like some suburban soap opera star with an evil twin who came out after car-pooling hours. I don't know what the root of Becky's intense dislike was; all I know is she's the first kid I ever heard scream, "I hate your stupid guts!" to a parent.

And that's really what scares me the most about going to Haiti this time. I can deal with muggers at the airport and the maddening red tape of the international adoption process, but I'm not sure how I'll handle it if Missy hates me. She's only met me once, and that was during a brief two-day visit nine months ago. Sure, a tutor is teaching her English using flash cards with pictures of me and her future home in Nashville, so every time she sees a picture of me now she squeals, "Mama!" But as much as that thrills my heart, I know it's mainly a learned response. Plus, since Skittles often accompany her correct answers, I think hers might be more of a sweet tooth connection than an emotional one. At best she remembers me as the big white stranger who brought presents. Like Santa, only with wider hips.

All my adoptive mom friends have encouraged me to go into this visit with low expectations. To not be surprised if Missy seems shy or anxious or even screams and acts out when she sees me. I understand it will be scary for her to leave the safe and familiar arms of her caretaker. It's going to be a huge transition for her when she realizes the large Santa lady is in her life to stay. However, I know all that *cognitively* because I've read a library full of books about adoption over the last few years, but my heart has always tended to dawdle behind my head. And my heart hopes she likes me.

In case you were wondering, I was able to peel myself off of the amorous couple on the Miami leg of my trip this morning, catch the connecting flight, and make it out of the Port-au-Prince airport relatively unscathed. I did end up being surrounded by multiple scammers and hooligans outside the baggage claim area, but fortunately most of them were petite. I think they sensed I could take them, so all but one backed off. His name was Joseph, and because he didn't stare at me like a lion eyeing a baby antelope on the Discovery Channel, I let him roll my bag to the parking lot and gave him ten bucks—way more than a good day's pay for most people in this inferno of a country.

Then I got into an SUV Joseph gestured to and climbed in the front seat next to a gentleman who nodded when I asked, "Are you from New Life Link?" Of course, in less than a mile I realized he didn't speak a word of English except, "Yes." But, at that point, what was a sleep-deprived, pale girl to do except buckle my seatbelt? We proceeded to career through the craziest traffic scenario I've ever experienced. Downtown London, New York City, and even Nairobi seem like rural Pennsylvania highways dotted with an Amish buggy or two by comparison. Bumper to bumper takes on a whole new meaning here. Plus, there are people hawking everything from mangos to used tires between the bumpers. And that chaotic cacophony of people, squealing breaks, and piles of burning trash was all going on in that same blistering heat that made me promise Jesus to become a missionary again if He'd just make a gallon of iced water or a Slurpee miraculously appear (oops, now you know it was me the first time too).

But maybe the heat was God's grace on this second visit, because it drained most of the worry from my soul until I was a dazed, sweaty lump of *c'est la vie*. Limp enough to relinquish the mirage of control and let whatever God allowed to be that week *to be.* In fact, I wasn't even sure I was in the right car until we pulled up to a building with bars over the windows and the hand-painted sign that I recognized as the Haitian arm of my adoption agency. But since my driver smiled the whole time, I thought even if he was taking me to a back alley where I'd become fodder for *CSI*'s new Port-au-Prince franchise, at least he was a pleasant escort.

When I was six years old, my Dad Harper took me and my new stepmother and stepbrother out for Carvel ice cream on a Friday night. I remember that night well for two reasons. One being that it was my first time to go to a Carvel, and I was excited because I'd never been to such a fancy ice cream store. We only had a Dairy Dip in our town at that time, and it was kind of run-down with big cracks in the vinyl seats and stuff like that. So going to Carvel with all those shiny pink plastic chairs, gleaming linoleum floors, and happy ice cream servers in matching outfits was not unlike the first time I walked into Nordstrom . . . it was awesome!

The second reason I remember that night with Dad and Luci and Ricky so well is that after we finished our ice cream, we got into Dad's Volkswagen Beetle and drove to an apartment complex around the corner, which is where I spent my first night with them away from home. It was a two-bedroom apartment, and because Ricky seemed a little perturbed about sharing his room with *a girl*, Dad made a pallet for me on the living room floor when it was time for bed. I told him that it was fine and I really liked sleeping on pallets.

I was lying.

The only time I'd ever slept on a pallet before that was once or twice when I'd gotten scared during a bad lightning storm and mom had fixed one for me right next to her bed. Then I liked it because I could hear mom breathing above me, so I knew everything was going to be okay even if the electricity had gone out. It wasn't the same feeling in a strange apartment after Dad patted me gruffly on the head and closed his and Luci's bedroom door firmly behind him. It wasn't the same thing at all. So I waited until the apartment got really quiet and was fully aware that I couldn't hear my mom breathing next to me. Then I cried.

I'm sitting on a twin bed in a guesthouse nestled in the hills of Haiti right now, listening to a two-year-old wail. He's been crying on and off since I got here yesterday.

As best I can tell, he's barely eating or talking, mostly he just wails mournfully. I know this because they have the room right next to mine. "They" are a really nice family who've come to Haiti to adopt him—to give this baby love and hope and health beyond what would probably be his future if he remained an orphan here. But as compassionate and consoling as this family of five has been toward him, they are still very, very different than the nannies at the orphanage he's used to. Right now, I don't think his toddler heart can comprehend how wonderful it will be to belong to a family. All he knows is that they're different. And change is hard.

> *Jesus, please help me to be brave and flexible. I'm so excited about becoming Missy's mama. I want to be the safe place she runs to when the electricity goes out in her life. I want to be the person breathing above her pallet. But I'm a little scared of what's ahead. And I'm sure she is too. Because "us" will be so very, very different than what we're used to.*

Fifteen hours have passed since the whole feminine-hygiene-product fiasco, but it feels more like fifteen months! "Smith"—one of the young men who works for New Life Link—and I spent the better part of Tuesday and Wednesday waiting for officials to see us and sign documents at the US Embassy, at Haiti's "low court" (which, until recently, took place under a palm tree in Port-au-Prince), and at Haiti's "high court" (which now takes place in the old American Embassy Building, complete with bathrooms that would make a trucker blush). And, of course, all the while we're waiting in that oppressive heat that has caused me to offer myself up as a living sacrifice twice now.

Unfortunately, we didn't even have the privilege of rolling down the windows in the cramped quarters of low court or high court like we did in traffic. In addition, the attire for court is dressy (Haitians take going to any type of government office very seriously, unlike the people I stand behind in line every year in the US while waiting to get my car tag renewed, who are obviously wearing pajama pants even if they were marketed as "lounge wear" at Target). So, in an effort to not come across as disrespectful and jeopardize my chances of getting the adoption petition signed, I, too, was wearing a nice skirt and blouse. Both became insufferable as the minutes turned into hours and the synthetic-fabric part of the "cotton-blend" began to melt uncomfortably into my flesh.

....

Thankfully, before I was permanently disfigured, the judge showed up and signed my papers without any fanfare. After almost a year of filling out, copying, and scanning enough paperwork to choke and kill a new printer (seriously), one man merely nodded in my direction and signed a single document and *whoosh*, the hardest part of the adoption process was complete! I was tempted to yell, "Yeehaaw!" and commence happy dancing, but there were serious men with serious guns watching me. So, instead, I said, "*Mesi boukou, monsieur*" and walked demurely out of his office as my heart started the cha-cha-cha.

But once we were outside the building, I high-fived Smith, gave a war whoop, and danced an abbreviated Latin jig while he laughed and said, "Oh no, Leeesa!" Then he put his hands teasingly over his face, a little embarrassed by my middle-aged-American-mama exuberance in an otherwise sedate setting! We proceeded to the street, where he hailed a taxi to go back to the office and wait for my ride to Neply to see Missy.

Before I go any further, I feel compelled to explain the difference between a Haitian taxi and an American, British, Canadian, or any other industrialized nation's version of a cab. In Haiti, taxis are neither yellow, nor owned and operated by a corporation. There are no special licenses, driver's tests, or vehicle regulations. The only thing required to be a taxi driver here is to own or have access to a car that runs. Well, actually, the "running" part isn't really a requirement, either! The fact that Smith was actually able to hail a car with *four* wheels instead of a two-wheeled "moto" (it's common to see two, or even three, people clinging to each other while perched precariously on the back of a small motorcycle, whipping wildly through traffic) was no small miracle.

However, after getting out of the US Embassy, low court, and high court with the necessary stamps and signatures officially authorizing me to continue the process of becoming Missy's mama, I could've cared less that our "cab" was an ancient compact car with no AC and seats without any upholstery. Instead, there was just a slab of foam with the springs poking through to plop my happy rear on. I also didn't mind when two sweaty, odiferous Haitian men squeezed into the backseat next to me, squashing me against the door that didn't lock or open from the inside (it was one of those reach-through-the-window-and-open-it-from-the-outside models).

All I could think was, *We've made two giant leaps forward in this journey of adoption, and there's just a few more to go until I get to bring my baby home!* However, I will admit it was a tad humiliating when our cabbie had to pull over and have air pumped into the left rear tire (the one directly beneath me and my springs) because the undercarriage kept scraping the road when we went over bumps.

After a short visit at the adoption agency, where I promised iPhones, iPods, imported chocolate, and anything else I thought might be motivating to Smith and his cohorts if they'd commit to seeing that the rest of my paperwork on the Haitian side got turned in on time (bribes are *strictly* prohibited at New Life Link because it is a well-run Christian agency, so these were simply tokens of my appreciation), I piled into that diesel-belching school bus for a second time and began the bone-jarring, two-and-a-half-hour drive to Neply to see Missy. The now-familiar harmony of car horns and squealing brakes accompanied us the whole way while my sweat formed a warm puddle beneath me. Yet I was surprisingly content. Somewhere in my very-hot-natured and not-typically-keen-about-public-transportation soul, I knew this was all just part of the crazy ride toward the holy grail of motherhood.

As soon as the bus lurched around the bend in front of the My Life Speaks main building in Neply, I started scanning the crowd for Missy. Within a few minutes, she came walking up shyly in a little pink dress holding Fifi's hand. I had to restrain myself from diving for her like a college co-ed lunging for beads in a Mardi Gras parade. But my mama-sense kicked in, so instead I smiled and calmly squatted down to her level and let her approach me because it had been so long since we met the first time. I don't have words to wrap around what I felt when she ran forward, wrapped her skinny brown arms around my neck, and said, "I lub you, Mama." Once again I knew what it felt like to have my heart toddling around outside of my body.

We spent the afternoon playing with some of the loot I unveiled one item at a time. And it became quickly apparent that Missy *loves* music and shoes. In fact, she literally squealed with glee and began to dance every time I played her a new song on my iPhone. Then I couldn't help but laugh when she jumped up and down and clapped her hands when I pulled a pair of tiny purple shoes out of my suitcase. I thought, *Yep, this is my kid, because that's exactly how I feel every time I get a new pair of shoes!* That sentiment was sealed during lunch the next day when she wet her index finger and pressed it onto her plate and then into her mouth over and over again so as to get every last crumb of her potato chip portion.

The next thirty-six hours were filled with heartwarming firsts for us: the first time we went for a really long walk and held hands the whole time; the first time she animatedly tugged me toward something she wanted to show me; the first time a villager asked if I was her mom in Creole and she said, "*Oui*" nonchalantly as we strolled by; the first time she put her hands on both sides of my face and said, "*Mesi, Mama*" after I picked her up when she stumbled; the first time she hid behind me when a stray dog came trotting toward us; the first time she fell asleep against my chest; the first time she submerged both hands gleefully into my hair, obviously intrigued that the texture is so different from hers; and the first time she placed a wad of half-chewed food that she no longer wanted into the palm of my hand.

But there were some heartbreaking firsts too. Like when we were driving back to Neply after visiting someone in a neighboring village and I looked down at her sitting quietly beside me to see tears streaming down her face and dripping off her chin. Or when she cried and turned her face away when she saw me again after I sent her home for a much-needed nap with the caretakers and surroundings she's used to. Or when she grunted and said, "No!" when Fifi tried to get her to sit beside me at dinner later that night. Or especially when her big brown eyes locked on mine with an expression of fear. That about killed me.

As I've already stated, I know it's normal for her to be apprehensive and anxious. I am too. However, I have forty-five more years of life experience than her, so most of the time I can reason that whatever change lies ahead, it won't kill me. She doesn't have the luxury of perspective. All she knows is three and a half years of life inside one square mile of a rural village, with limited indoor plumbing, sporadic electricity, and simple, infrequent meals outside of the New Life Speaks campus. Purple shoes, iPods, potato chips, and affectionate "blan" (white) mamas can all but overload her heart and mind.

So I scooted down the bench several feet away from Missy and didn't attempt to interact with her while she shot me wary sideways glances every minute or so. And when Fifi pushed her toward me insistently (because she's afraid I'll back out of adopting Missy if she misbehaves, leaving them destitute and unable to provide Missy with the HIV meds she needs), I reassured her through an interpreter that I was committed to *all of them*—to her, Missy, and Missy's maternal grandmother—and I wasn't backing out, I was just backing up. We explained that this was a massive transition for Missy and she needed time and space to adjust so that she could move back toward me when she felt more comfortable and secure.

Eventually (thankfully), within an hour, she did. Relief doesn't begin to describe what I felt when she cautiously climbed into my lap after dinner, leaned her head against my chest, and sighed. My entire being exhaled anxiety right along with her. I am forever magnificently ruined.

10

CARNIVOROUS COMMODES, TOWERING CLIFFS, AND THE LIBERATING LOVE OF CHRIST

Do all the good you can,
By all the means you can,
In all the ways you can,
In all the places you can,
At all the times you can,
To all the people you can,
As long as you ever can.[1]

—*John Wesley*

U sing the term *plumbing* to describe the convoluted arrangement of PVC pipes, latrines, and cisterns that are all somehow connected to a muddy stream in Missy's village is a huge disservice to the word itself. Furthermore, the primitive nature of their sanitation system, combined with the fact that there's only one well for the entire village, causes the water pressure to fluctuate so much that the few working toilets burp and bubble continuously like porcelain volcanoes. They also overflow with enthusiastic regularity, and since all of the facilities are interdependent, the sinks and showers fill up with whatever caused the commode to cough. I've been to a lot of underdeveloped countries and I've used many a Port-O-Let on camping trips and at concert venues, but I've never experienced anything as disquieting as going to the restroom in Haiti.

Nevertheless, around lunchtime on the second day of my recent visit with Missy, I decided she surely needed to "go potty" since she'd had a lot of fluid since breakfast. So I said, "Come on, Sweetie, let's go inside to the bathroom." I was pleased when she willingly took the hand I offered and meandered along merrily beside me. However, the merriment ended as soon as she saw the toilet. She backed away from it like it was some terrible beast, poked out her bottom lip, and was unconvinced that all would be well, in spite of the gentle tone I used while unbuttoning her shorts and getting her situated on the throne.

Of course, I thought her potty-phobia was typical for a toddler, because a lot of my friends' small children in America aren't fond of toilets either—especially if they don't have that "child-seat" on top and the poor things have to hang on to the rim for dear life to keep from falling through! So I knelt down in front of the toilet and held Missy firmly and kept saying soothingly, "I've got you, honey . . . you're not going to fall in . . . it's okay . . . Mama's got you . . . please go pee pee, sweetie." I wasn't sure how many words she understood except for the term "pee pee," which is the same in Creole as in English.

What I didn't know is that while Missy is technically potty-trained, she's actually never used "inside facili- ties" before. And just when she finally got comfortable, squinched her eyes and wrinkled her darling nose in a concentrated effort to "go," the toilet erupted with a fero- cious roar and shot a geyser of water all over her and me! She shrieked in terror, and I snatched her up as fast as I could while slipping and sliding in my flip-flops on the wet tile floor. She clung to me fiercely and buried her face in my neck, whimpering. So I just rubbed her back and repeated over and over, "Shush baby, I've got you. Mama's got you. It's okay."

She stopped crying pretty quickly but kept her little arms and legs wrapped tightly around me, which cata- pulted me to cloud nine with the thought, *She feels safe with me!* But then the happy fog lifted and I crash-landed back into reality when it occurred to me that she's likely to still be in Pull-Ups when she starts middle school because it's going to be a long, long time before she's ever going to be comfortable around a commode!

The older I get, the more I think comfort is overrated. Especially if you're a believer. Paul certainly didn't seem concerned about it when he encouraged the believers in Corinth to be *all in* with this sermon:

> Do you not know that in a race all the runners run, but only one gets the prize? Run in such a way as to get the prize. Everyone who competes in the games goes into strict training. They do it to get a crown that will not last, but we do it to get a crown that will last forever. Therefore I do not run like someone running aimlessly; I do not fight like a boxer beating the air. No, I strike a blow to my body and make it my slave so that after I have preached to others, I myself will not be disqualified for the prize. (1 Corinthians 9:24–27 NIV)

I can definitely relate to the whole "striking blows to the body" discomfort necessary to compete in a foot race. In fact, I still have scars from the half marathon my almost-little-brother Kyle Cooksey talked me into running last spring. It's called the Music City Half Marathon, and Kyle's smart wife and my dear friend Laura managed to *conveniently* be on tour with Mandisa the weekend the race was scheduled. So when Kyle found out that I was going to be in town that weekend after all due to the cancelation of a speaking engagement, he slipped into salesman mode to try and convince me why it was such a great idea for me to join him in a masochistic sweat-fest.

I'm still not sure why I agreed to it. I used to run 10Ks when I lived in Colorado, and not only did I never win a top-place medal, bad words usually flickered across the screen of my mind from the starting gun to the finish line because I was so miserable. I'm just not built for long-distance running. I'm more the short-distance type. Two or three miles at a comfortable trot and I'm a happy camper. But, like I said, Kyle is basically my little brother and he was just so stinkin' persuasive that before I knew it I was downtown at the Nashville Convention Center signing up to run with thirty-two thousand other nutters.

While I was standing in line to pay the registration fee and get one of those big paper numbers you have to pin to your shirt for the race, I was concerned one of those officials walking around in a matchy-matchy Nike shirt was going to walk up and say, "Ma'am, we can tell you're not capable of running 13.1 miles like a fleet-footed gazelle because we noticed your cellulite from across this crowded lobby. So why don't you just back away from the table before somebody gets hurt." But they didn't. In fact, I noticed quite a few other Ben & Jerry's fans while I was waiting and thought, *Hey, my sturdy tribe is representing, baby! We're gonna to do this thing!* After swiping my credit card and wincing because the receipt revealed an amount equivalent to a pair of really cute shoes, I wandered over to the merchandise area. I figured if I was going to run thirteen miles, I at least wanted the T-shirt to prove it.

While I was standing in line to pay for a T-shirt . . . and a nice fuzzy fleece . . . and a super-cute running skirt, something else caught my eye. At first I thought it was deodorant, but then I got close enough to read the label and decided I simply *had to have* Mission Skincare's Long-Lasting Anti-Chafe Balm! A chipper, sing-song voice in my head squealed happily, *Where have you been all my life, Balmy? Do you know how many forest fires we could've prevented if you'd been kind enough to coat my inner thighs during my past attempts at long-distance running?*

I bought two sticks, just in case I decide to wear a skirt again the next time I'm in Haiti.

Unfortunately, no one told me that it'd be a good idea to reapply the balm around mile marker six or seven during the race. So, in spite of owning one of the greatest innovations the sporting world has ever known, I still ended up with a painful rub-burn (Remember when we used to do "Indian burns" on each other's arms in middle school? What in the world was that all about?), which left a faint ribbon of raised, white scars high on the inside of each thigh.

The bottom line is this: it's a safe assumption that running all out so as to win the spiritual prize Paul talks about will cause us at least a twinge of discomfort!

I don't think it's by chance that this book is due tomorrow and I find myself writing the last chapter today, March 31, 2013 . . . Easter Sunday. It feels gloriously fitting to enthuse about running full speed, taking big risks, *overextending for the cause of Christ* on this, of all days. The day Jesus-followers around the world are focusing on the earth-shaking miracle of the empty tomb!

Although my eyelids are droopy because I went to bed at two a.m. after writing most of the night and then got up at five thirty to attend our church's sunrise service, my heart is raring to go! Especially in light of one small half-verse that jumped out at me when Pastor Steve taught from this passage in Matthew 27 at seven a.m. to several hundred hearty Tennesseans sitting outside in a muddy field by the river, in folding chairs we'd lugged across the parking lot, in the drizzling rain:

....

Now from the sixth hour there was darkness over all the land until the ninth hour. And about the ninth hour Jesus cried out with a loud voice, saying, "Eli, Eli, lema sabachthani?" that is, "My God, my God, why have you forsaken me?" And some of the bystanders, hearing it, said, "This man is calling Elijah." And one of them at once ran and took a sponge, filled it with sour wine, and put it on a reed and gave it to him to drink. But the others said, "Wait, let us see whether Elijah will come to save him." And Jesus cried out again with a loud voice and yielded up his spirit.

And behold, the curtain of the temple was torn in two, from top to bottom. And the earth shook, and the rocks were split. The tombs also were opened. And many bodies of the saints who had fallen asleep were raised, and coming out of the tombs after his resurrection they went into the holy city and appeared to many. When the centurion and those who were with him, keeping watch over Jesus, saw the earthquake and what took place, they were filled with awe and said, "Truly this was the Son of God!" (Matthew 27:45–54, emphasis mine)

I've been a Christian for a really long time now, since long before Mark Zuckerberg was even born, and I've never thought much about how the temple curtain was torn in half when Jesus allowed His body to be broken on that hill called Calvary. I mean, I've sung songs about it and stuff, and even used the phrase a few times when I was teaching about how New Testament believers have immediate access to Jesus instead of signing our power of attorney over to a high priest we've never even had coffee with, who only got to enter the Holy of Holies one day a year on our behalf. But I've never considered how honkin' (My sister hates it when I use that word because she thinks it makes me sound like a redneck. And I guess the shoe fits, since I willingly sat in a muddy field and happily belted out worship choruses led by a bluegrass band before listening to Pastor Steve preach this morning) *HUGE* that curtain actually was!

According to ancient rabbinical literary sources, it was the exact dimensions of the American flag that now flies over Ground Zero in Manhattan. But it was much, much heavier—probably several thousand pounds—because it was as thick as a man's hand and it took up to three hundred people to move it:

> The Veils before the Most Holy Place were 40 cubits (60 feet) long, and 20 (30 feet) wide, of the thickness of the palm of the hand, and wrought in 72 squares, which were joined together; and these Veils were so

heavy, that, in the exaggerated language of the time, it needed 300 priests to manipulate each. If the Veil was at all such as is described in the Talmud, it could not have been rent in twain by a mere earthquake or the fall of the lintel.[2]

Plus, it was *torn in two, from top to bottom*, at the ninth hour (v. 46), which meant this massive, two-inch-thick piece of fabric ripped in half, causing an enormous crash at three o'clock in the afternoon, right about the time the temple priests were standing in front of it, dutifully doling out sticks of incense and going through the motions of religion. I bet they were *way* more startled than Missy was during her first potty experience! No wonder the book of Acts reports that a slew of them got saved:

> The word of God was continuing to spread. The group of followers in Jerusalem increased, and a great number of the Jewish priests believed and obeyed. (Acts 6:7 NCV)

That whole veil-splitting-down-the-middle drama disconcerted those priests right into discipleship!

I've been thinking about how that colossal rip led to revival all day. And I can't help marveling at the huge, heavy things God has torn from my life to bring about revival too. Things like fear and insecurity and shame so thick I was emotionally exhausted just from hauling it around everywhere I went.

So when I sat down with my laptop this afternoon to finish this book, here's what I prayed:

> *Lord Jesus, thank you so much for the glorious freedom you bought for me with your blood. And thank you for continuing to tear down strongholds like resentment and anxiety in my life. If anyone besides my immediate family reads this, please use this imperfect prose to help rip off the unnecessary burdens they're lugging around as well. I pray they will be light enough to take whatever leap of faith you've called them to.*

Much to classy Theresa's chagrin, I grew up an All-American tomboy. I was more likely to be found climbing a tree than playing with Madame Alexander dolls. And my favorite playground of all was Dad's forty-two-acre farm out in the country (our parents divorced when Theresa was eight and I was four). It was a Central Floridian paradise of rolling hills—perfect for racing dirt bikes—and large swathes of woods—perfect for pretending to be Pocahontas. Dad also kept a herd of docile black-and-white

Herefords, which I thought had the potential to be great foils for a game I made up called Psych the Cows.

The rules of Psych the Cows was simple: I'd grab a coffee can full of sweet feed from the barn (because that's what Dad used to coerce the cows in for dinner) and then I'd cajole my stepbrother, Ricky, into leaving his beloved Atari game and go outside to the main pasture with me. After helping him get settled into one of the big oaks in a copse of trees near where the cows grazed, I'd trot out to the edge of the thicket, shake the feed can vigorously, and mimic the way Dad beckoned our four-legged milk machines.

That was usually all it took to tempt the cows to gallop in our direction. And if I kept shaking the can and singing the "cows come hither" refrain long enough, sometimes it would turn into a full-fledged stampede, which was my hope. Because it was absolutely thrilling to outrun our bovine posse and swing up into the tree beside a terrified Ricky mere seconds before being flattened, and yell "Psych!" as fifty or sixty cows thundered underneath us!

Of course, cows aren't as dumb as they look, and quickly clued into the fact that I wasn't going to feed them. So the game only worked once or twice a weekend. Which is why one Saturday, after a stirring round of nearly-being-trampled, I turned to Ricky and said enthusiastically, "Let's go psych the bull!" Ricky, who was not nearly as prone to daredevil activities as I was, blanched and replied, "No way, Lisa! Your dad told us not to go anywhere near that bull because he's super dangerous!"

I knew Ricky was right. I knew the pawing, snorting, wild-eyed Texas Longhorn sequestered on our north pasture was sinister. I knew I should probably amble back up to the house and do my homework instead of provoking twelve hundred pounds of would-be ribeye. But I couldn't help thinking that as exciting as being chased by cows was, how much more exhilarating it would be to get charged by a big, scary bull.

So I used my best negotiating skills and reasoned with Ricky that there was *no way* we'd get hurt since my plan involved us entering the bull's habitat at a place where we'd be guaranteed at least a hundred-yard head start to escape. I insisted the bull probably wouldn't even notice us because his usual grazing spot was so far away from where we were going to sneak under the barbed wire.

My guess is that while thirty-seven years have passed since that fateful weekend romp, Ricky's probably still miffed at how very wrong I was! Instead of placidly chewing grass in the sun one hundred yards away from our entry point, that maniacal hunk of beef was lurking behind a tree in the shadows mere feet from where we crawled under the fence. And before I could think, much less shake the feed can, he came charging toward us with his giant neck angled so that his horns would have maximum impact.

I whirled around and took off sprinting toward the fence, noticing that my long-suffering stepbrother—who'd been dragging his feet about ten or fifteen yards behind me—had already escaped without a scratch. My white-hot fear was tinged with relief for a second—*at least Ricky wasn't going to maimed because of me!* But then I had to focus on my own survival. I ran like heck and somehow managed to stay a few feet in front of the bull until we got to the fence. I leapt onto a post, my feet firmly planted on the barbed wire on either side, poised to vault safely out of his territory. Unfortunately, the U-shaped nail holding the top strand of barbed-wire in place was loose, so when I jumped on it to spring to freedom, it popped out of the post and the barb sliced up the back of my thigh and wedged into my bottom—effectively skewering me in place.

Contrary to popular belief, my twelve years of life did not flash before me. Nor did I see a beautiful white light beckoning me toward a long tunnel. I did not feel one iota of peace. What I felt was the giant head of a really mad cow trying to butt me off my high-wire act. What I saw were his horns thrusting into thin air on either side of me. And what flashed before me was the sobering thought that I was surely going to be grounded until the age of thirty! Thankfully, before that speedy slab of beef could figure out how to orient his massive horns so as to gore me, Dad came racing up from the barn, pushed the bull backward, and hoisted me off the fence and into his arms. Other than a nasty scar running up the back of my right thigh (which is yet another reason I'm not prone to wear bikinis or Daisy Duke cut-offs), the most significant souvenir of that day is the question Dad asked while driving me to the doctor to get stitches: *Was it worth it?*

Hmmm. Was it worth it? Was the unprecedented exhilaration, adrenaline rush, spine-tingling fear, and narrow escape from certain death to a joyous appreciation for the life I got to keep worth it? Yes, unreservedly, *YES!*

While my adolescent penchant for racing cows reveals that sometimes I'm not the sharpest tool in the shed (as if you had any doubts by now), I have grown to appreciate every single scar etched into my jar of clay because they prove I put myself out there. I've taken risks. I didn't sit idly on the curb while life passed me by. I'm learning to do the same thing with my heart. If it gets a little dinged in the overextension process, it just proves I trusted Jesus enough to put it out there. Besides, I think God digs chicks with scars. And I'm cool with that . . . as long as they don't come from carnivorous commodes.

I'd like to wind down by thanking you very much for buying my book. It means a lot to me, especially if you're not one of my first cousins. But in case you're tempted to purchase another one for a friend or something, I want to encourage you to buy Ian Morgan Cron's latest tome, *Jesus, My Father, the CIA, and Me* instead, because he writes with a loveliness that I can only dream of possessing someday.

My favorite story he's written (and I apologize for being somewhat of a literary spoiler here) has to do with how his eight-year-old son, Aidan, faced his fears and leapt off a forty-foot cliff into the dark water of a quarry below, which forced Ian's heart to stretch too. It goes like this:

> *Aidan looked over the side, took a deep breath, and blew out. Then he looked at me and said again, "I mean it, Dad. If you jump, so will I."*
>
> *The next thing that happened made me believe that maybe some of the more fantastic Bible stories are really true. Maybe the power of the Lord can embolden a kid to kill a giant with a sling-shot. Maybe grace can make a rascal noble or a coward brave even if it's only for a moment.*
>
> *I walked off the ledge.*
>
> *The college kids were wrong. It was four full arm*

revolutions before I hit the water. The drop was high enough that the impact hurt the bottom of my feet. A belly flop from this height would liquefy your internal organs. But it was exhilarating as all get-out. I was twelve again.

But then I remembered Aidan.

I looked up to see my eight-year-old boy, peering down at me. Around him was the Greek chorus of lacrosse players, fascinated by the family drama playing itself out in front of them. What I realized as I looked up at Aidan was just how high this jump really was and how letting him make the leap might be a really bad idea. He was so small. What if he landed wrong and did some serious damage to his neck or back: What if he accidentally hit a slab of marble no one knew was just below the surface? What if a condor snatched him midair and took him to its aerie to feed him to its condor babies? These are the kinds of things that go through my mind even now as an adult.

Aidan smiled at me, and I knew in my heart that everything in his life and in mine had always been leading up to this moment. He jokingly made the sign of the cross three times fast and then jumped. Like his sisters, he hit the water so perfectly that his entrance into the water barely disturbed the surface.

'Yes!" I cried and waited for him to come up.[3]

. . . .

I believe that's essentially what God wants for each one of us as well. For us to leap off our towering cliffs of fear, uncertainty, shame, anxiety, resentment, and religious propriety into the crystal-blue sea of extravagant faith in Jesus and compassion for others, because we just *know* our Divine Dad is in the water below, waiting for us.

ACKNOWLEDGMENTS

Lisa would like to thank the following ministries and organizations for providing divinely orchestrated opportunities for her—and many of her friends—to be joyfully overextended:

The Next Door, Inc. is a faith-based, nonprofit residential transitional program dedicated to serving women in crisis, equipping them for lives of wholeness, and hope.

www.thenextdoor.org

myLIFEspeaks is a ministry that was launched in 2012 by Mike and Missy Wilson, who felt compelled to provide a campus home and care for special needs children who have been orphaned and abandoned in Haiti.

www.mylifespeaks.com

....

Live Beyond is a faith-based, nonprofit humanitarian organization, which serves third world countries by building hospitals, purifying water, and providing microfinance. The founders, Dr. David and Laurie Vanderpool, recently sold their successful medical practice in Brentwood, Tennessee, and moved to Thomazeau, Haiti, to do the work God has called them to full-time.

www.livebeyond.org

The Fellowship of Christian Athletes is an interdenominational Christian sports ministry whose vision is to see the world impacted for Jesus Christ through the influence of athletes and coaches.

www.fca.org

NOTES

Chapter 1

1. Judith Valente and Charles Reynard, *Twenty Poems to Nourish Your Soul* (Chicago, IL: Loyola Press, 2006), 3.
2. *Hebrew-Greek Key Word Study Bible* (Chattanooga, TN: AMG Publishers, 1996), 2066.
3. William Hendriksen, *New Testament Commentary: Luke* (Grand Rapids, MI: Baker, 1978), 594.
4. Craig A. Evans and Stanley E. Porter, editors, *Dictionary of New Testament Background* (Downers Grove, IL: InterVarsity Press, 2000), 1056–60.

Chapter 2

1. Bob Goff, *Love Does* (Nashville, TN: Thomas Nelson, 2012), 25.

Chapter 3

1. Brené Brown, *Daring Greatly* (New York: Penguin, 2012), 2.

Chapter 4

1. Tim Hansel, *When I Relax I Feel Guilty* (Colorado Springs, CO: David C. Cook, 1979), 22.

....

2. Lisa Harper, *Malachi: A Love That Never Lets Go* (Nashville, TN: LifeWay Press, 2012).
3. *www.planecrashinfo.com*
4. Tom Scheve, "How many muscles does it take to smile?" Discovery Fit & Health (2011). DataFace, "Facial Expression: A Primary Communication System." (May 14, 2009). Waller, Bridget M.; Cray, James J., Burrows, Anne M. "Selection for Universal Facial Emotion" (2008).

Chapter 5

1. Mary Karr, interview by Dean Nelson, Writer's Symposium by the Sea Sponsored by Point Loma Nazarene University, February 16, 2011, accessed June 4, 2012, www.youtube.com/watch?v+t9qYvJF7qx0&.
2. C. S. Lewis, *The Four Loves* (New York: Houghton Mifflin Harcourt, 1991), 121.

Chapter 6

1. Madeleine L'Engle, *Walking on Water: Reflections on Faith and Art* (Colorado Springs, CO: WaterBrook Press, 2001).
2. Dr. Francis Schaeffer and C. Everett Koop, *Whatever Happened to the Human Race?* (New York, NY: F.H. Revell, 1979).
3. Alastair Hannay, ed., *Kierkegaard: Concluding Unscientific Postscript* (Cambridge, UK: Cambridge University Press, 2009).
4. Dr. Francis Schaeffer, *The Francis A. Schaeffer Trilogy: The Three Essential Books in One Volume* (Wheaton, IL: Crossway Books, 1990), 45–46.
5. Dr. Francis Schaeffer, *The God Who Is There* (Downers Grove, IL: InterVarsity Press, 1998).
6. G. K. Chesterton, *Orthodoxy* (San Francisco: Ignatius Press, 1995; reprinted from John Lane Company, 1908).

7. Blaise Pascal, *Pensees* (London, England: Penguin Books, 1966).
8. C. S. Lewis, *C. S. Lewis: Life, Works, and Legacy* (Westport, CT: Praeger Publishers, 2007), 278.

Chapter 7

1. Craig Groeschel, *The Christian Atheist* (Grand Rapids, MI: Zondervan, 2010), 54.
2. Tim Keller, *The Prodigal God* (New York: Penguin, 2008), 49–50.
3. Brené Brown, *Daring Greatly* (New York: Penguin, 2012), 125.
4. Ibid., 126.

Chapter 8

1. R. Ralph William Franklin, ed., *The Poems of Emily Dickinson* (Boston: Harvard University Press, 2005), 329.
2. www.cdc.gov/HIV/topics/basic.

Chapter 9

1. Brennan Manning, *Ruthless Trust* (New York: HarperCollins, 2000), 1.

Chapter 10

1. John Wesley, George Eayrs, Augustine Birrell, *Letters of John Wesley* (London: Hodder and Stoughton, 1915), 423.
2. Alfred Edersheim, *The Life and Times of Jesus the Messiah*, http://cbumgardner.wordpress.com/2010/04/06/the-thickness-of-the-temple-veil.
3. Ian Morgan Cron, *Jesus, My Father, the CIA, and Me* (Nashville, TN: Thomas Nelson, 2011), 241–42.

ABOUT THE AUTHOR

Rarely are the terms hilarious storyteller and theological scholar used in the same sentence, much less used to describe the same person . . . but then again, Lisa Harper is anything but stereotypical. She has been lauded as a gifted communicator, whose writing and speaking overflows with colorful, pop-culture references that connect the dots between the Bible era and modern life. Her style combines sound scriptural exposition with easy-to-relate to anecdotes and comedic wit.

Her vocational resume includes six years as the

director of Focus on the Family's national women's ministry where she created the popular Renewing the Heart conferences, attended by almost 200,000 women, followed by six years as the women's ministry director at a large church in Nashville. Her academic resume includes a masters of theological studies with honors from Covenant Seminary in St. Louis. Now a sought-after Bible teacher and speaker, Lisa is currently featured on the Women of Faith tour and speaks at many other large multi-denominational events—such as Moody Bible, Women of Joy, and Focus on the Family conferences—as well as at hundreds of church retreats all over the world. She's been on numerous syndicated radio and television programs and was featured on the cover of *Today's Christian Woman*.

She's written ten books including *Holding Out For a Hero: A New Spin on Hebrews*; *A Perfect Mess: Why You Don't Have To Worry About Being Good Enough For God*; and *Untamed: How the Wild Side of Jesus Frees Us to Live and Love With Abandon*. Lisa's latest book is titled *Stumbling Into Grace: Confessions of a Sometimes Spiritually Clumsy Woman*. She also served as a key contributor to the Becoming Devotional Bible for Women and as a columnist for *Today's Christian Woman* magazine.